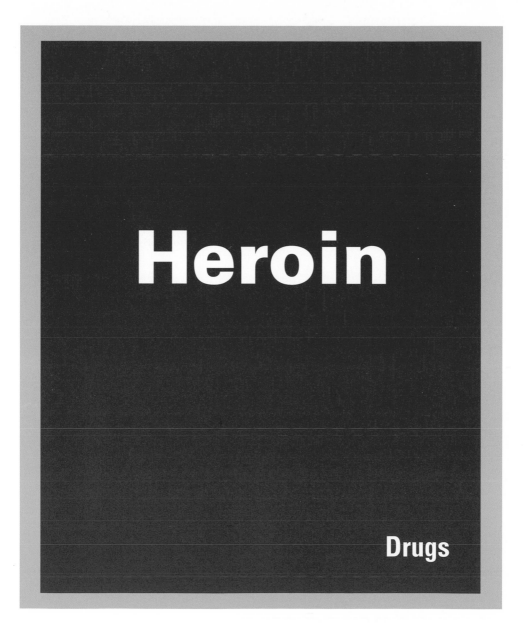

Heroin

Drugs

Other books in the Compact Research series include:

Drugs
> Marijuana
> Methamphetamine
> Nicotine and Tobacco
> Performance-Enhancing Drugs

Current Issues
> Biomedical Ethics
> The Death Penalty
> Gun Control
> Illegal Immigration
> World Energy Crisis

COMPACT *Research*

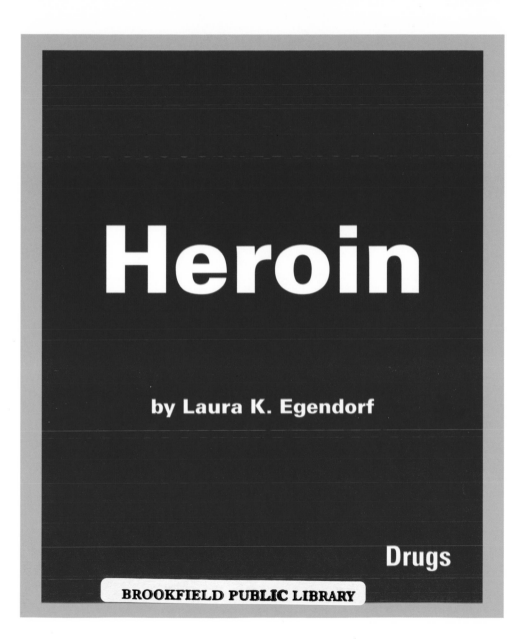

Heroin

by Laura K. Egendorf

Drugs

ReferencePoint
Press™

San Diego, CA

© 2007 ReferencePoint Press, Inc.

For more information, contact
ReferencePoint Press, Inc.
PO Box 27779
San Diego, CA 92198
www. ReferencePointPress.com

Picture Credits:
AP/Wide World Photos, 11
Steve Zmina, 28–31, 42–44, 57–60, 71–73

Series design:
Tamia Dowlatabadi

LIBRARY OF CONGRESS CATALOGING-IN-PUBLICATION DATA

Egendorf, Laura K., 1973–
  Heroin / Laura K. Egendorf, author.
    p. cm. — (Compact research series)
    ISBN-13: 978-1-60152-002-9 (hardback)
    ISBN-10: 1-60152-002-6 (hardback)
    1. Heroin. 2. Heroin abuse. 3. Heroin abuse—Prevention. 4. Heroin abuse—Treatment. I. Title.
  HV5822.H4E44 2006
  362.29'3—dc22
                                      2006031259

Contents

Foreword

> ❝ Where is the knowledge we have lost in information? ❞

—"The Rock," T.S. Eliot

As modern civilization continues to evolve, its ability to create, store, distribute, and access information expands exponentially. The explosion of information from all media continues to increase at a phenomenal rate. By 2020 some experts predict the worldwide information base will double every seventy-three days. While access to diverse sources of information and perspectives is paramount to any democratic society, information alone cannot help people gain knowledge and understanding. Information must be organized and presented clearly and succinctly in order to be understood. The challenge in the digital age becomes not the creation of information, but how best to sort, organize, enhance, and present information.

ReferencePoint Press developed the Compact Research series with this challenge of the information age in mind. More than any other subject area today, researching current events can yield vast, diverse, and unqualified information that can be intimidating and overwhelming for even the most advanced and motivated researcher. The Compact Research series offers a compact, relevant, intelligent, and conveniently organized collection of information covering a variety of current and controversial topics ranging from illegal immigration to marijuana.

The series focuses on three types of information: objective single-author narratives, opinion-based primary source quotations, and facts and statistics. The clearly written objective narratives provide context and reliable background information. Primary source quotes are carefully selected and cited, exposing the reader to differing points of view. And facts and statistics sections aid the reader in evaluating perspectives. Presenting these key types of information creates a richer, more balanced learning experience.

For better understanding and convenience, the series enhances information by organizing it into narrower topics and adding design features that make it easy for a reader to identify desired content. For example, in *Compact Research: Illegal Immigration*, a chapter covering the economic impact of illegal immigration has an objective narrative explaining the various ways the economy is impacted, a balanced section of numerous primary source quotes on the topic, followed by facts and full-color illustrations to encourage evaluation of contrasting perspectives.

The ancient Roman philosopher Lucius Annaeus Seneca wrote, "It is quality rather than quantity that matters." More than just a collection of content, the Compact Research series is simply committed to creating, finding, organizing, and presenting the most relevant and appropriate amount of information on a current topic in a user-friendly style that invites, intrigues, and fosters understanding.

Heroin at a Glance

Prevalence

More than 10 million people worldwide use heroin.

Health Effects

Heroin use can result in numerous diseases, in particular those that are spread through the sharing of dirty needles. Nearly a quarter million Americans have AIDS as a result of injection drug use.

Crime

A disproportionate number of criminals are on or have recently used heroin at the time of their arrest. In addition, in 2005, U.S. law enforcement arrested 2,038 people on heroin-related charges.

Prevention

Many argue that early education, such as the Drug Abuse Resistance Education (D.A.R.E.) program, can prevent young people from using heroin or other drugs. More than 36 million children around the world have taken part in the D.A.R.E. program.

Treating Heroin Addiction

Methadone is the most common treatment (used by 40 percent of heroin addicts who receive treatment), but it can be inconvenient to use.

Needle Exchange Programs

These controversial programs enable heroin addicts to receive clean syringes in order to reduce the spread of AIDS and other communicable diseases. There are one 185 needle exchange programs in the United States.

Decriminalization

Opponents of current drug laws governing heroin believe that people possessing a small amount of heroin should not be imprisoned or receive any other criminal penalty.

War on Drugs

The U.S. government spends $20 billion annually to reduce the spread of illegal drugs. Opponents contend that the war on drugs increases crime while failing to decrease drug use.

Overview

"Call it smack. Or H. Or skag or junk. By any name, heroin is dangerous, addictive, and illegal."

—John DiConsiglio, "Close-Up: Heroin," *Science World,* April 18, 2003.

Drugs are one of the most dangerous problems facing America and the rest of the world. One especially harmful drug is heroin. More than 10 million people use heroin worldwide. According to the U.S. National Survey on Drug Use and Health, 3.7 million Americans have used heroin at least once. The Monitoring the Future Study, which is conducted by the Institute of Social Research at the University of Michigan each year, reported that 1.5 percent of eighth, tenth, and twelfth graders have used heroin at least once in their lives and 0.5 percent had used it during the previous 30 days. In total, about 1 million Americans are addicted to heroin and an estimated 13 to 18 metric tons of heroin are consumed in the United States each year.

This use is not limited to urban and poor areas, which most people associate with drug addiction. Heroin users also live among the middle class and in suburbs and small towns. During the 1990s, for example, Plano, Texas, a city of 222,000 approximately 17 miles from Dallas, was devastated by a series of 16 heroin overdoses. Unfortunately, the problem appeared to be reemerging in 2005 and 2006, as 3 teenagers overdosed in Plano and the surrounding area.

The Social Dangers of Heroin Use

Illegal drug use is sometimes thought of as a victimless crime, but the truth is that drugs, heroin in particular, have a troubling impact not only

This heroin was found by German police during routine truck control procedures. Authorities confiscated one hundred kilograms in the seizure.

on the user but also on society as a whole. A heroin habit can cost an addict up to ten thousand dollars per year, depending on how much heroin he or she uses each day. In order to afford such a habit, many addicts commit crimes such as robbery or prostitution. As a result, heroin is a burden on the criminal justice system, with more than 87,000 drug offenders in federal prisons at a cost of more than $20,000 per person per year. Heroin addicts also often find themselves withdrawing from family and friends and unable to hold jobs as their drug use increases.

The Physical Effects of Heroin Use

A dose of heroin is one-tenth of a gram and typically costs between 5 and 10 dollars. The purity of Colombian heroin ranges from 80 to 90 percent, but heroin that is sold on the street is frequently mixed with other substances, including other drugs or baking powder, which significantly reduces its purity. Because a heroin user can never be certain of the purity of the heroin he or she is taking, it can be easy to inject, smoke, or swallow a dose that is too pure, which can lead to an overdose.

As their addiction continues, heroin users build up a stronger tolerance to the drug. This means that they must take a larger dose of heroin in order to experience its effects. A larger dose increases the chance of an overdose.

> "As their addiction continues, heroin users build up a stronger tolerance to the drug."

Heroin users take the drug because they enjoy its immediate effects—relaxation and a "rush," or a pleasurable sensation; however, these effects are short-term, and the continued use of heroin causes many unpleasant consequences. Heroin addicts experience a wide variety of physical ailments, among them skin infections, organ damage, and a higher risk of contracting diseases that are spread through the sharing of needles; for example, AIDS and hepatitis. They lose weight at a rapid and unhealthy rate and often have to dress in unseasonably warm clothes in order to hide the "tracks," or injection sites, that appear on their skin from repeated heroin injections. Women who use heroin while pregnant are at a greater risk for miscarrying or giving birth to addicted children. Heroin use can also lead to overdosing, which is often fatal. Heroin addicts are frequent outpatients at hospitals; in 2004 there were 162,137 heroin-related visits to the emergency room.

Heroin also affects addicts when they try to kick the habit. Withdrawal symptoms, which can include nausea and muscle cramps, are sometimes too painful for addicts to bear. They would often rather risk illness or death through heroin use than go through withdrawal. Withdrawal symptoms are also psychological in nature, with addicts experiencing depression, anxiety, and mood swings. According to the *Encyclopedia of Mental Disorders,* "The individual who is dependent on opioids [such as heroin] has difficulty imagining living without the drug, since they were dependent on it to function. This is similar to how someone addicted to nicotine may feel after giving up cigarettes."[1]

Heroin and Its History

Heroin is part of a class of drugs known as opiates. Other drugs in this class include opium, codeine, and morphine. These drugs are derived from the opium poppy. Opiates are used as painkillers; however, even the opiates that have legitimate uses can be addictive because people become dependent on the painkilling effects. By 1906 the medical community had acknowledged that heroin was twice as addictive as morphine, a painkiller that had been in use since the early 1800s. The U.S. government acknowledged the danger of heroin by restricting its distribution in 1914 under the Harrison Narcotics Act and banning its distribution altogether in 1924.

How Heroin Is Made

Heroin is derived from raw opium gum, a product of the opium poppy. The gum is removed from the plant and then dried. Then the gum is dissolved in boiling water. Next, the liquid is drained and filtered. What remains after the substance is dried is morphine. Heroin is created by boiling morphine and acetic anhydride over a stove, a process first discovered in 1874 by English chemist C.R. Wright. Two decades later, Heinrich Dreser, a researcher at the Bayer pharmaceutical company, tested the effects of this new drug on animals and other employees. Bayer began selling the drug commercially in 1898 under the name "heroin," so called because it made its users feel heroic. The company stopped producing heroin in 1913.

> " By 1906 the medical community had acknowledged that heroin was twice as addictive as morphine. "

The Heroin Trade

Heroin use may be illegal in the United States, but that has not prevented it from being brought into and sold within the country. The heroin trade is an international endeavor because the countries that produce heroin for the most part are not the same countries where it is used. In 2004, 632 metric tons of heroin were produced, 582 of those tons in Afghanistan. The other major producers of heroin are Burma, Thailand, Laos, Pakistan, Mexico, and Colombia. Mexico and Colombia provide most of the heroin used in the United States, Mexico to states west of the Mississippi and Colombia to the eastern United States, with the remaining amount produced in Asia. Sixty percent of heroin in the United States arrives from Colombia. Afghanistan's heroin is sent primarily to Europe, reaching it through a route across the Balkans.

> **Mules [drug couriers] swallow condoms or balloons filled with heroin and excrete them upon crossing the border.**

Heroin is smuggled by air and sea to the United States and elsewhere via the use of drug "mules," or couriers. Former Drug Enforcement Administration (DEA) agent Felix J. Jimenez, in testimony before a congressional committee in December 2002, reported that the average courier smuggles in 5 to 8 kilograms, or approximately 11 to 17 pounds, of heroin per shipment. Mules swallow condoms or balloons filled with heroin and excrete them upon crossing the border. They are paid an average of $5,000 per trip, but with that money comes the possibility of arrest or even death. If the balloon or condom bursts during the trip, the mule may die of an overdose.

Drug traffickers do not rely exclusively on people to transport heroin. One drug smuggling operation, thwarted in February 2006, used puppies. The smugglers placed liquid heroin packets inside purebred puppies. Three of the dogs died while six others survived the attempted smuggling. As drug traffickers devise new ways to sneak heroin into the United States, America's government and the governments of other nations affected by heroin have to keep pace to stop smuggling operations.

The Violent Consequences of the Heroin Trade

The heroin trade is dangerous for reasons beyond the distribution of drugs. Drug trafficking, especially in Colombia and Afghanistan, helps finance terrorism. The United Nations has reported that terrorist groups receive hundreds of millions of dollars from narcotics sales, while the Drug Enforcement Administration has identified 17 foreign terrorist organizations that have possible ties to the global drug trade, including al Qaeda, the group behind the September 11, 2001, terrorist attacks. In testimony before the House of Representatives, Thomas W. O'Connell, an assistant secretary of defense, detailed how terrorist groups can take advantage of the drug trade:

> Poppy cultivation and the revenues generated from different aspects of narcotics trade provide fresh resources for extremists and terrorists. The infrastructure of smuggling that supports narcotics trafficking also services terrorist transportation and logistics needs. Local leaders and commanders can use profits from narcotics to oppose a unified Afghan government that hopes to provide full security to its citizens.[2]

Rogelio E. Guevara, the chief of operations for the DEA, told the House Committee on Government Reform, "Colombia's . . . terrorist organizations, the National Liberation Army (ELN) and the United Self Defense Forces of Colombia (AUC), are . . . believed to be engaged in the drug trade to support their terrorist agendas. The FARC [Revolutionary Armed Forces of Colombia] and AUC derive roughly 70 percent of their operating revenues from narcotics trafficking."[3] The heroin trade also funds crimes other than terrorism in Turkey, the Balkans, and West Africa.

Another crime linked to the heroin trade is police corruption. Police and detectives, especially those who work in the narcotics division, may find themselves tempted to start selling the drugs in order to supplement their incomes or to demand that dealers give them free drugs in exchange for hiding illegal activi-

> **Terrorism and other crimes associated with the heroin trade are unlikely to decline.**

ties. One example of drug-related police corruption in the United States occurred in Los Angeles, where a deputy sheriff and two police officers committed home invasion robberies under the guise of legitimate investigations and stole valuables and drugs. Mexico is another country where the police have become part of the drug world. Ian Vásquez writes for the libertarian think tank the Cato Institute that "President Vicente Fox's arrest of hundreds of police officers on drug-related charges is only the latest confirmation that the illicit industry has managed to corrupt government officials at all levels."[4]

Unfortunately, terrorism and other crimes associated with the heroin trade are unlikely to decline. Many of the nations most affected by heroin are either opposed to U.S. foreign policy, such as Iran, or lack the financial resources to fight the spread of heroin, such as Burma and Thailand. The U.S. federal government spends only $20 billion on the War on Drugs, a pittance compared with what it spends on defense.

A Worldwide Problem

As its effects—both on the individual drug user and society as a whole—indicate, heroin is a dangerous worldwide problem. Compact Research: *Heroin* looks at heroin in the following chapters: How Dangerous Is Heroin? How Can Heroin Use Be Prevented? Are Treatments for Heroin Addiction Effective? Should Heroin Use Be Decriminalized or Legalized? The material presented in this book will provide a reader with a greater understanding of the impact heroin has on society.

How Dangerous Is Heroin?

❝ Heroin is a highly addictive drug, and its abuse has repercussions that extend far beyond the individual user.❞

—National Institute on Drug Abuse, Research Report Series, "Heroin Abuse and Addiction," May 2005.

Heroin is one of the world's most addictive drugs—in fact, only nicotine has been found to be more addictive. Dependence on heroin develops quickly because its effects on the brain are immediate. Users immediately notice how heroin affects their bodies and, liking the results, find that they need to continue taking the drug in order for those effects to continue. A one-time experience with heroin can quickly become a potentially deadly addiction, with the addict needing to shoot up more heroin each time as he or she builds up a tolerance to the drug. As their dosages increase, heroin users are at greater risk of succumbing to the many dangerous side effects of the drug.

How Heroin Is Taken

Heroin users take the drug in four ways. The most common form is injection into veins or subcutaneously (beneath the surface of the skin). Heroin can also be snorted, smoked, or swallowed. Some users mistakenly believe that as long as they do not use a needle they will avoid any of the drug's dangerous effects; however, that belief is incorrect. Regardless of how heroin users take the drug, they are at risk for its many harmful consequences.

The Physical Effects of Heroin

The first part of the body affected by heroin is the brain. Heroin enters the brain quickly, where it attaches to opioid receptors. Opioids that are naturally produced by the body regulate hunger and thirst and help control moods and the body's immune system; this class of chemicals also includes endorphins and dynorphin. Because heroin is also an opioid, it can attach to receptors and thereby affect the entire body and change the way a user feels. According to Alan I. Leshner, director of the National Institute on Drug Abuse, heroin has several physiological effects, including slowing down respiration, depressing the heart rate, and reducing pain. Heroin also can create sudden pleasurable sensations, or a "rush." The drug's ability to reduce pain is one reason why many people use heroin. For example, the late rock star Kurt Cobain stated that he used heroin to help relieve the agony of stomach pains.

> Some users mistakenly believe that as long as they do not use a needle they will avoid any of the drug's dangerous effects.

The brain is not the only organ affected by heroin. Continued heroin use causes significant damage to the liver, heart, and lungs. Potential problems include infected heart linings and valves, pneumonia and other pulmonary problems, and liver disease. Addicts frequently lose significant amounts of weight and develop an unhealthy pallor. Another danger is that heroin is never completely pure but is instead mixed with other substances, from baking soda and flour to other drugs. If the additives are not dissolved completely by the body, blood vessels that lead to the organs can become clogged, leading to infections.

Diseases and Death

Because they often share needles instead of using clean needles for each injection, heroin users are also more vulnerable to a variety of infectious diseases such as AIDS and hepatitis. As of 2004, according to the Centers for Disease Control and Prevention, 248,813 Americans have been diagnosed with AIDS due to injection drug use. Sixty percent of new cases of hepatitis C are the result of sharing needles or using dirty needles, while 17 percent of instances of hepatitis B occur among injection drug users. Other diseases associated with shared needle use include endocarditis, a form of heart infection, and wound botulism, a disease that can cause paralysis and death. Should an addict attempt to end his or her habit, the physical symptoms of withdrawal—nausea, chills, and muscle cramps—can also be overwhelming.

Even beyond the damage to organs and the heightened risk of certain diseases, heroin use tends not to coexist with a healthy lifestyle. Heroin addicts tend not to eat well or take care of their bodies in general, thereby causing damage to their bodies that has nothing directly to do with the drug itself. For example, an addict who has to turn to prostitution in order to pay for a heroin habit risks exposure to sexually transmitted diseases and sexual assault.

The most dangerous effect of heroin use is overdosing. Heroin users overdose when they take more heroin than their body can handle. Instead of merely slowing down the user's heart rate and respiration, this larger dose of heroin causes the user's body to shut down completely. People who overdose can sometimes be revived, but death is the typical result—1,793 Americans suffered a fatal heroin overdose in 2001, according to the Centers for Disease Control and Prevention. A major reason why heroin overdoses occur is that users can never be sure how pure the heroin they are using is. If a user's body has developed a tolerance to heroin that is 40 percent pure, injecting an equivalent amount of 70 percent pure heroin can prove deadly.

> " Sixty percent of new cases of hepatitis C are the result of sharing needles or using dirty needles. "

It is not always the user who experiences the effects of heroin. Children can be born addicted to heroin if their mother used the drug while pregnant. These children are also at greater risk for sudden infant death syndrome (SIDS) and develop more slowly than do children who were not exposed to heroin in the womb. Studies have shown, however, that there are no significant lasting differences between children who had addicted mothers and those who did not.

Psychological and Social Effects

Heroin not only affects the body—it is harmful psychologically as well. Addiction is both physical and psychological in nature because heroin users begin to feel that they must take the drug regularly in order to cope with life; however, as heroin addicts continue to use the drug they often become depressed and start to feel helpless. The depression might lead to suicide, as heroin addicts are 14 percent likelier to commit suicide than nonaddicts. If an addict attempts to stop using heroin, withdrawal symptoms such as anxiety and mood swings can cause such agony as to make the person restart his or her addiction. When combined with the physical symptoms of withdrawal, the discomfort can be too hard to bear. According to James Tighe, a health expert for the British Broadcasting Corporation, the psychological effects of withdrawal are often ignored, much to the detriment of addicts. "For most addicts, their problem is a mixture of both physical and psychological aspects. There are some instances when it's difficult to distinguish between the two."[5]

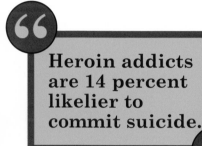

Heroin addicts are 14 percent likelier to commit suicide.

Heroin also affects society in negative ways. Family members and friends must deal with the possibility of a loved one dying of an overdose or of the addict becoming depressed, withdrawn, or associating only with other users. Heroin addicts also often steal from those close to them in order to pay for their habit. People outside the addict's inner circle may also become crime victims; 3.3 percent of male arrestees and 4 percent of female arrestees admitted to using heroin during the previous week, according to the National Institute of Justice. The trade and distribution of heroin is also fraught with violence, with drug dealers killing each other in order to increase their share of the market.

Questioning the Dangers of Heroin

Not everyone agrees that heroin is inherently dangerous, however. Some people who doubt the reported dangers of heroin argue that it is not heroin that is the problem but rather that it becomes dangerous when combined with alcohol or other drugs, such as cocaine (a combination known as a speedball). The drugs that are mixed with heroin before it reaches the users can also prove deadly. In addition to damaging the organs, as previously noted, these drugs can cause overdoses. In spring 2006 more than 400 people in Philadelphia, Detroit, and Chicago died after taking heroin that was laced with fentanyl, a painkiller that is eighty times more powerful than morphine. Stanton Peele, who has written extensively on what he considers the myths surrounding drugs and alcohol, details this theory in his article "The Persistent, Dangerous Myth of Heroin Overdose." He writes,

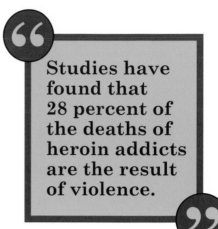

"Studies have found that 28 percent of the deaths of heroin addicts are the result of violence."

> The majority of drug deaths in an Australian study, conducted by the National Alcohol and Drug Research Centre, involved heroin in combination with either alcohol (40 percent) or tranquilizers (30 percent). If it is not pure drugs that kill, but impure drugs and the mixture of drugs, then the myth of the heroin overdose can be dangerous.[6]

The health-related problems caused by heroin use have also been questioned. One alternative theory that has been offered is that heroin users do not become sick from the drug itself but instead from the lifestyle that surrounds drug addiction. Heroin users can become malnourished if they spend the bulk of their money on drugs instead of food. If the addiction keeps them from holding a job, they may not have health care; the diseases associated with heroin addiction can worsen as a result. The violence that accompanies drug addiction, namely the crimes that are committed in order to buy and sell heroin (an addiction can cost as much as 10 thousand dollars per year), is particularly deadly. Studies have found that 28 percent of the deaths of heroin addicts are the result of violence.

Heroin Use Affects All of Society

Most people consider heroin to be a dangerous drug that leads to addiction and other physical, psychological, and social problems. The effects of heroin addiction impact not only the drug users but all of society.

Primary Source Quotes*

How Dangerous Is Heroin?

❝Drug use causes people to commit crime, making neighborhoods less safe and less secure for our families. Drugs help supply the deadly work of terrorists.❞

—President George W. Bush, remarks on the 2002 National Drug Control Strategy, February 12, 2002.

Bush is the forty-third president of the United States.

....

❝Heroin addiction is really a lifestyle. Once users cross the line (into dependency), they use the drug every day.❞

—Karen Miotto, "Heroin Treatment: An Interview with Dr. Karen Miotto," www.drugstory.org.

Miotto is an associate professor at the University of California at Los Angeles School of Medicine.

....

* Editor's Note: While the definition of a primary source can be narrowly or broadly defined, for the purposes of Compact Research, a primary source consists of: 1) results of original research presented by an organization or researcher; 2) eyewitness accounts of events, personal experience, or work experience; 3) first-person editorials offering pundits' opinions; 4) government officials presenting political plans and/or policies; 5) representatives of organizations presenting testimony or policy.

66 I started using heroin when I was fifteen. I began using it to come down from cocaine and get some sleep.
But I started liking the heroin high and started using
it straight. 99

—Erica, "Chasing the High: An Interview with Erica," www.drugstory.org.

Erica is the pseudonym of a teenager who told her story to DrugStory.org, a Web
site developed by the National Youth Anti-Drug Media Campaign.

66 Despite its reputation . . . heroin is neither irresistible
nor inescapable. Only a very small share of the population ever uses it, and a large majority of those who
do never become addicted. 99

—Jacob Sullum, "H: The Surprising Truth About Heroin and Addiction," *Reason,* June 2003.

Sullum is the senior editor and a columnist for the magazine *Reason*.

66 Injection drug use has been associated directly or in-
directly . . . with more than one-third of AIDS cases in
the United States. 99

—National Institute on Drug Abuse, "Research Report: HIV/AIDS," March 2006. www.nida.nih.gov.

The National Institute on Drug Abuse supports research on drug abuse and addiction.

❝Once a junkie, always a junkie. You can stop using junk [heroin], but you are never off after the first habit.❞

—William S. Burroughs, *Junky: The Definitive Text of "Junk,"* Fiftieth anniversary edition. New York: Penguin, 2003.

Burroughs wrote *Junky,* a memoir about his life as a heroin addict.

❝When [heroin users] take whatever they can off the street, they have no way of knowing how the drug is adulterated.❞

—Stanton Peele, "The Persistent, Dangerous Myth of Heroin Overdose," *Drug Policy Forum of Texas News,* August 1999.

Peele is a psychologist who has written extensively on addiction.

❝Snorting or smoking heroin is more appealing to new users because it eliminates . . . the fear of acquiring syringe-borne diseases, such as HIV and hepatitis.❞

—Drug Enforcement Administration, *Drugs of Abuse,* 2005. www.dea.gov.

The DEA enforces America's drug laws.

❝A third of [heroin addicts] rely on illegal activities, such as drug dealing and manufacture, property crime and commercial sex, to buy drugs and make a living.❞

—Office of National Drug Control Policy, *The Economic Costs of Drug Abuse in the United States, 1992–2002,* December 2004. www.whitehousedrugpolicy.gov.

The ONDCP establishes the policies of America's drug control program.

❝ It's important to remember that there's often more to an addiction than the physical withdrawal symptoms. ❞

—James Tighe, "Drug Use and Addiction," August 2006. www.bbc.co.uk.

Tighe is a health expert for the British Broadcasting Corporation and a clinical nurse research fellow.

❝ Drugs are far more addictive than alcohol. . . . Only 10 percent of drinkers become alcoholics, while up to 75 percent of regular illicit drug users become addicted. ❞

—Drug Enforcement Administration, "Speaking Out Against Drug Legalization," May 2003. www.dea.gov.

The DEA enforces America's drug laws.

How Dangerous Is Heroin?

- An average of 5 percent of heroin addicts die each year.

- In 2004 the Drug Abuse Warning Network reported that 162,137 visits to hospital emergency rooms were heroin related.

- Heroin use is often linked with crime. The National Institute of Justice reported in 2004 that 3.3 percent of arrested men and 4 percent of arrested women had used heroin during the previous week.

- Twenty percent of tenth graders, according to the 2005 Monitoring the Future Survey, report that heroin is "fairly easy" or "very easy" to obtain.

- Thirty-five percent of people who try heroin are at risk of becoming dependent on the drug.

- Americans who have been diagnosed with AIDS due to injection drug use number 248,813.

- Ninety percent of injection drug users have at least one infectious disease.

- Heroin users who inject the drug experience its effects within eight seconds.

Heroin's Effects on the Brain

The effects of heroin on the brain are felt immediately. All physical pain is dulled or totally relieved within seconds as the "rush" takes hold of the user. Addicts need to use increasing amounts of the drug as tolerance builds, often times overstimulating the brain.

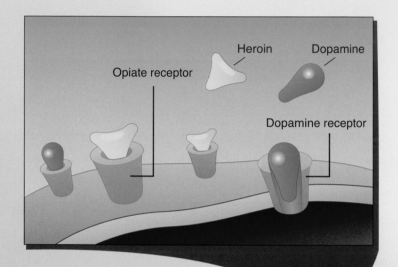

Heroin binds to opiate receptors on brain cells in several parts of the brain. This stimulates the production and increased release of dopamine, a chemical thought to induce feelings of pleasure.

The Limbic System
Controls emotions and feelings of pleasure. Heroin acts here to produce an intense rush, which addicts seek compulsively.

The Brain Stem
Controls basic bodily functions, like heartbeat and breathing. Heroin can restrict respiratory function to the point that the user stops breathing and dies.

In the Spinal Cord
Heroin has a pain-relieving effect. It blocks pain messages between nerve cells so a user will feel little pain.

Source: *Scholastic*, "Heroin," John DiConsiglio, 2006.

Effects of Heroin Use

This table shows the long- and short-term effects heroin can have on a user. While long-term use is thought to be most detrimental to health, a user can die the very first time trying heroin.

Short - Term Effects	Long - Term Effects
"Rush"	Addiction
Depressed respiration	Infectious diseases
Clouded mental functioning	Collapsed veins
Nausea and vomiting	Bacterial infections
Suppression of pain	Abscesses
Spontaneous abortion	Infection of heart lining and valves
	Arthritis and other rheumatologic problems

Source: NIDA, "Heroin Abuse and Addiction Research Report," May 2005. www.nida.nih.gov.

- Approximately 62 percent of heroin users inject the drug.

- Marijuana use is 45 times more prevalent than heroin use.

- According to HeroinAddiction.info, over 80 percent of heroin users inject with a partner, yet 80 percent of overdose victims found by paramedics are found alone.

- The average heroin dependent person uses between 150 to 250 milligrams per day, divided into 3 doses.

- The average heroin addict spends between $100 to $200 a day to support their heroin addiction.

- According to the Drug Abuse Warning Network heroin and morphine accounted for 51 percent of drug deaths ruled accidental or unexpected in 1999.

Injecting Heroin Declines While Rehab Admissions Increase

While using heroin in any capacity is dangerous, the most dangerous method of use, injection, is on the decline in the United States. Inhalation is becoming more popular among users because they wrongly believe that snorting heroin will help them avoid the health problems associated with injecting the drug.

Heroin Rehab Admissions

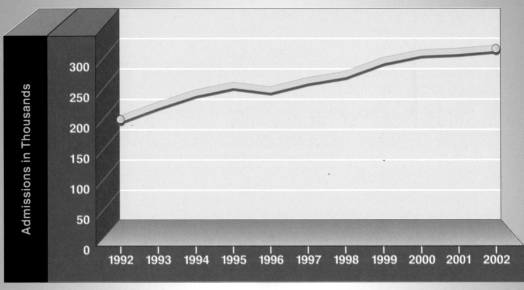

Heroin Injections Are Declining

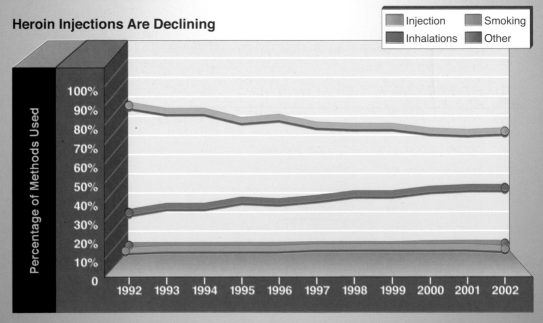

Source: National Drug Intelligence Center, "National Drug Threat Assessment 2006," January 2006.

Heroin Contributes to the Spread of AIDS

This chart shows that the second and third leading cause of AIDS transmission is directly related to using needles to inject drugs. Heroin is the most widely injected drug, although injection use is declining.

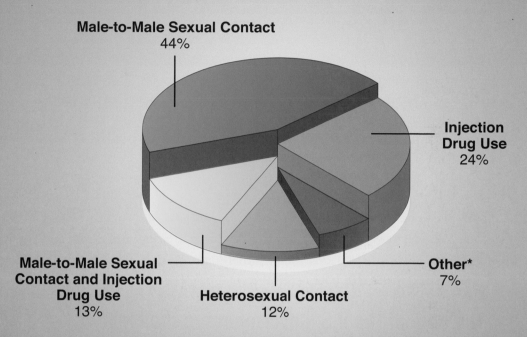

Male-to-Male Sexual Contact
44%

Injection Drug Use
24%

Male-to-Male Sexual Contact and Injection Drug Use
13%

Heterosexual Contact
12%

Other*
7%

*Includes Hemophilia/coagulation disorder; receipt of blood transfusion, blood components or tissues, and other risk factor, and risk factor not reported or identified.

Source: Centers for Disease Control and Prevention and United States Department of Health, "HIV/AIDS Surveillance Report, 2004," www.hivwebstudy.org.

- Major withdrawal symptoms peak between 48 and 72 hours after the last dose and subside after about a week.

- According to NIDA, in Newark, NJ, 82 percent of drug treatment admissions (excluding alcohol) in 2004 were attributable to primary heroin abuse.

How Can Heroin Use Be Prevented?

"It is . . . important to continue to educate young people about the dangers of drug use and build a cultural norm that views illicit drug use as unacceptable."

—The Office of National Drug Control Policy, "Stopping Drug Use Before It Starts," 2006.

Several issues surround the prevention of heroin use in the United States. These issues include stopping the sale of heroin, discouraging heroin use by using the criminal justice system, and educating children about the effects of heroin.

The Role of the U.S. Government in the Fight Against Heroin

The federal government aims to prevent drug users from gaining access to heroin in three ways: by stopping the shipment of heroin into the United States, stopping distribution within the United States, and working with other countries to end the production of heroin. None of these approaches has been completely successful, as Americans continue to buy and use heroin.

The government agency that plays the largest role in the fight to prevent heroin use is the Drug Enforcement Administration (DEA). According to its Web site, www.dea.gov, the mission of the DEA is to "enforce the controlled substances laws and regulations of the United States."[7] It has enjoyed many successes in thwarting the distribution of heroin in the United States. For example, in August 2006 the DEA announced the arrests of 138 people involved in an international operation to sell black tar heroin in the United States. The administration also seized 17 kilograms of the drug. Two months earlier, drug enforcement agents, with the help of Colombian authorities, toppled a $25 million heroin ring and arrested 56 people. The DEA has also ended a smuggling operation in which heroin was hidden in car batteries and transported from Guatemala to Mexico and the United States. This DEA operation, nicknamed Operation Jump Start, led to the arrests of more than 100 people and the seizure of more than 22 kilograms of heroin. In 2005 the DEA seized 639 kilograms of heroin.

The United States has worked with the governments of major heroin-producing nations to stop the production of the drug. Two of these nations are Colombia and Afghanistan. In 1999 the government of Colombia introduced Plan Colombia, a $7.5 billion program whose goals included fighting the nation's powerful narcotics industry. In a gesture of support, the United States has offered $1.3 billion in assistance to Colombia. The amount of heroin grown in Colombia has decreased since the plan's inception. In 2001 Colombia grew 6,540 hectares of opium poppies, which produced 4.3 metric tons of heroin. Only 2,100 hectares were cultivated in 2004.

The success of Plan Colombia has been disputed, however. One criticism is that the plan focused more on the eradication of coca plants than on poppy plants. As a result, Congressman Dan Burton of Indiana has charged in a hearing on the plan, "[There] has been an increase in Colombian heroin available in the United States, an increase in hospital admissions for overdoses and an increase in overdose deaths in nearly every big city and small town east of the Mississippi."[8] Other critics have raised humanitarian concerns, asserting that Plan Colombia has increased violence between Colombia's government and drug-trafficking guerrillas and that the herbicides used to destroy poppies have also ruined food crops.

> " The government agency that plays the largest role in the fight to prevent heroin use is the Drug Enforcement Administration (DEA). "

Heroin Production in Afghanistan

The U.S. government, four months prior to the terrorist attacks of September 11, 2001, gave poppy eradication money to the Taliban, the fundamentalist

Islamic government that controlled Afghanistan before it was toppled following America's invasion of that nation after September 11. The U.S. government had provided $43 million in aid to the Taliban because of its efforts to ban the cultivation of poppies in Afghanistan. Antinarcotics efforts there have become largely ineffective since the end of 2001, however. Following the war in Afghanistan in late 2001 and the fall of the Taliban, heroin production in Afghanistan rose sharply, from 7 metric tons in 2001 to 150 metric tons in 2002. Afghanistan's reemergence as the world leader in heroin production was an unintended consequence of the war. This increase in heroin output has occurred because the Taliban is regaining power throughout the country, and instead of banning poppy crops Taliban leaders are now encouraging their cultivation. Militants associated with the Taliban are using profits from the heroin trade in order to purchase weapons.

Heroin and the Criminal Justice System

The U.S. government also aims to reduce heroin use by punishing those who use and sell the drug. The federal government determines the legal consequences for drug possession based on a drug's benefits and dangers; this is known as drug scheduling. Heroin is a Schedule I drug because it has a high potential for abuse and, unlike other opiates such as morphine, has no medical use. The penalty for heroin trafficking (manufacturing and distribution) varies based on the amount of heroin being transported. For a first offense of between 100 and 999 grams, a convicted trafficker will serve between 5 and 40 years in prison and face a fine of up to $2 million. For amounts of at least 1 kilogram, a life sentence is possible. The unlawful possession of heroin without intent to sell can result in up to 10 years in jail and a $100,000 fine. In 2005 U.S. law enforcement officers arrested 2,038 people on heroin-related charges. Despite these arrests, heroin use among adults has increased. During 2004, 398,000 Americans used heroin at least once, compared with 314,000 in 2003.

> "Following the war in Afghanistan in late 2001 and the fall of the Taliban, heroin production in Afghanistan rose sharply.

Educating Adolescents About Heroin

The best way to keep adults from using heroin may be to teach them about its dangers when they are young. Public service advertisements, or PSAs, can greatly influence drug use by teenagers. The Partnership for a Drug-Free America is a leading organization in the creation of these commercials, which use memorable images and dialogue to teach adolescents about the dangers of drugs and to remind parents that it is their responsibility to make sure their children are well informed about the deadly consequences of substance abuse. These PSAs have included imagery such as eggs frying in a pan to represent an adolescent brain on drugs. A study in the *American Journal of Public Health* of thirty antidrug advertisements found that PSAs are not as effective as their creators might hope, in large part because the commercials are underfunded and not broadcast enough to change the behavior of teenagers. At the same time, the authors write, students who viewed the PSAs and responded to a survey stated that most of the advertisements discouraged them from using drugs; however, the authors observe, "There were several that had little or no effect and 6 that had negative effects; that is, after viewing these 6 PSAs, the adolescents felt that they and their friends would be more likely to try drugs."[9] Antiheroin PSAs were among the most effective.

> Antidrug classes are another common way to teach students about heroin and other harmful substances.

Antidrug classes are another common way to teach students about heroin and other harmful substances. The most well known of these classes is Drug Abuse Resistance Education, better known as D.A.R.E. Founded in 1983, D.A.R.E. brings local police officers to classrooms to teach children how to resist peer pressure and stay away from drugs. D.A.R.E. has developed different curricula for elementary school, middle school, and high school classrooms, with each program building on the lessons learned in earlier sessions. Twenty-six million American children and 10 million in other countries have participated in the program. Studies indicate that the program is successful, including surveys of students in Texas and Louisiana that found that D.A.R.E. participants are less likely to try drugs and are more likely to talk to parents and teachers about drugs. One study by the University of Akron's Institute for Health and Social Policy has found that the police officers who lead the programs are at least as effective as teachers are in teaching about substance abuse.

Criticisms of D.A.R.E.

> **Student athletes are 40 percent less likely to turn to drugs.**

Many critics of D.A.R.E., however, contend that it has done little, if anything, to reduce the rate of drug use among teenagers. Studies, such as one conducted by the American Federation of Teachers, have found that students who participate in D.A.R.E. are no less likely to take drugs than students who do not participate. A writer for the *Oregonian* newspaper, citing another study critical of D.A.R.E., argues:

D.A.R.E, and other 'just say no' programs [referring to an antidrug slogan developed by former first lady Nancy Reagan] rely on hype over science when it comes to educating our kids.

Dr. Joel Brown of Berkeley-based Educational Research Consultants conducted the most extensive evaluations of drug education programs to date. His research, published in leading national scientific journals, showed that drug education programs are not only ineffective but may actually be hurting your kids.[10]

Another criticism of D.A.R.E. is that by using police officers instead of teachers or health-care professionals, the program places too much emphasis on the legal reasons why adolescents should not use drugs and may discourage youth from seeking help for drug-related health issues. Common Sense for Drug Policy, an organization that seeks to reform current drug laws, argues, "A police officer may intimidate adolescents who have experimented with drugs from asking lifesaving questions out of fear that they will get into trouble."[11]

An alternative to D.A.R.E. and other in-class programs are after-school programs. Studies conducted in the 1990s found that students who are involved in after-school programs, instead of spending time unsupervised, are less likely to use heroin. These programs can include after-school sports, volunteer work, or organized recreational activities. A 1995 study by the Search Institute, a nonprofit organization that provides information and resources to promote healthy youth, concluded that adolescents who perform volunteer work are 50 percent less likely to use drugs. Student athletes are 40 percent less likely to turn to drugs. After-school opportunities particularly benefit girls, especially if the programs are run by strong female role models who can help boost the girls' self-esteem. Girls often start using drugs during their teenage years because of low self-esteem and concerns about body image. The weight loss associated with heroin use may appeal to them; in the early 1990s the fashion industry was notorious for glamorizing heroin by using models who resembled addicts.

Parents Can Prevent Heroin Use

It is not solely the responsibility of schools and after-school programs to teach adolescents about the effects of heroin. Parents and guardians also need to talk to their children about why heroin use should be avoided. The Web site Parents: The Anti-Drug (www.theantidrug.com) advises parents to encourage their children to talk to them by showing interest in their children's lives and interests. The organization also suggests that parents try to be honest about their own drug use and teach their children how to resist peer pressure and turn down offers of heroin and other drugs. Additionally, parents and guardians should be aware of the signs of drug abuse, among them withdrawal from family and friends, a loss of interest in activities their children once enjoyed, and the disappearance of small amounts of cash. By the same token, parental neglect can lead to drug abuse, according to a study published in *Clinical Psychology Review* in 2002.

> **Parental neglect can lead to drug abuse, according to a study published in *Clinical Psychology Review* in 2002.**

Preventing heroin use requires Americans at all levels to work together, from the federal government to law enforcement to schools to parents; however, no hard data exists that any of these tactics has been completely successful. More efforts will likely need to be made in order to end heroin use in the United States.

Primary Source Quotes*

How Can Heroin Use Be Prevented?

“Kids who learn about the risks of drug abuse from their parents or caregivers are less likely to use drugs than kids who do not.”

—National Youth Anti-Drug Media Campaign, *Keeping Your Kids Drug-Free*, www.mediacampaign.org.

The campaign was created by Congress in 1998 to prevent and reduce drug use among America's youth.

“The Taliban is getting stronger from the billion-dollar narcotics backwash that floods enemy coffers.”

—Michael Yon, "Hooked," *National Review Online*, September 12, 2006. www.nationalreview.com.

Yon runs the blog www.michaelyon-online.com and is a contributor to *National Review*'s Web site.

* Editor's Note: While the definition of a primary source can be narrowly or broadly defined, for the purposes of Compact Research, a primary source consists of: 1) results of original research presented by an organization or researcher; 2) eyewitness accounts of events, personal experience, or work experience; 3) first-person editorials offering pundits' opinions; 4) government officials presenting political plans and/or policies; 5) representatives of organizations presenting testimony or policy.

66 The [Plan Colombia] policy so far has largely disregarded concerns about several important issues, including human rights abuses, . . . [and] the plight of Colombia's internally displaced population. 99

— Janice D. Schakowsky, statement, hearing before the House Committee on Government Reform, *America's Heroin Crisis, Colombian Heroin , and How We Can Improve Plan Colombia,* 107th Congress, 2nd session, December 12, 2002.

Schakowsky is an Illinois congressional representative.

66 We now know that we've made progress in cocaine and coca eradication in Colombia. We could do the same thing with heroin. 99

—Jon L. Mica, statement, hearing before the House Committee on Government Reform, *America's Heroin Crisis, Colombian Heroin, and How We Can Improve Plan Colombia,* 107th Congress, 2nd session, December 12, 2002.

Mica is a congressional representative from Florida.

66 If teens can make it to adulthood without experimenting with drugs, they are far less likely to begin using drugs later in life. 99

—White House, National Drug Control Strategy, February 2006. www.whitehousedrugpolicy.gov.

66 Because risks appear at every transition from infancy through young adulthood, [drug] prevention planners need to develop programs that provide support at each developmental stage. 99

—National Institute on Drug Abuse, *Preventing Drug Use Among Children and Adolescents: A Research-Based Guide,* March 1997.

NIDA, which is part of the National Institutes of Health, supports research on drug abuse and addiction.

❝Engaging young people directly about drug use has been shown to reduce the chances of drug initiation.❞

—Office of National Drug Control Policy, "Stopping Drug Use Before It Starts," 2006. www.whitehousedrugpolicy.gov.

The ONDCP establishes the policies of America's drug control program.

❝By combining grassroots PR—including T-shirts, bumper stickers and rallies—with aggressive political lobbying of local, state and federal governments, D.A.R.E has become its own special interest group.❞

—Kendra Wright, "Dare We Admit It? Drug War Is a Bust with Our Children," *Oregonian,* January 20, 1998.

Wright is the facilitator of FamWatch, a national network concerned about the effect drug policies have on families.

❝Five evaluations . . . found no significant differences between the DARE and non-DARE students over the long term.❞

—General Accounting Office, *Youth Illicit Drug Use Prevention: DARE Long-Term Evaluations and Federal Efforts to Identify Effective Programs,* January 15, 2003. www.gao.gov.

The GAO studies the programs and expenditures of the federal government.

❝I believe that if children respect law enforcement, and have positive role models available, they will in turn respect their parents, . . . more importantly themselves, by not using drugs.❞

—Don Roycraft, "D.A.R.E. Program Works to Help Kids Avoid Violence and Drug Use," *Colorado Springs Gazette,* October 21, 1999.

Roycraft is a D.A.R.E. officer.

Facts and Illustrations

How Can Heroin Use Be Prevented?

- Girls are less likely than boys to use heroin. While 3.8 percent of boys have used heroin at least once, only 2.5 percent of girls have done so.

- The average retail price for one gram of heroin in 2003 in the United States was between $60 and $400.

- In 2004 Mexico and Colombia produced a combined total of 12.4 metric tons of heroin. By comparison, Afghanistan produced 582 metric tons.

- The U.S. cities where heroin is principally distributed are Los Angeles, New York, Miami, Chicago, St. Louis, and Philadelphia.

- Eighty percent of U.S. schools have participated in the D.A.R.E. program since its inception in 1983.

- Sixty percent of the heroin used in America comes from Colombia.

- The Drug Enforcement Administration seized 639 kilograms of heroin in 2005.

- One hundred ten thousand metric tons of opiates were seized worldwide in 2003. Slightly more than half of that amount was heroin.

Heroin Seizures in the United States, 2003–2004

More than half of the heroin seizures in the United States took place in New York City airports. Restricting the supply of heroin into the United States is critical in reducing its usage.

Port of Entry	Heroin Seized (in KG)
New York, NY	738.96
Memphis, TN	178.26
Newark, NJ	159.01
El Paso, TX	110.36
Atlanta, GA	95.01
Laredo, TX	79.98
Washington, DC	78.11
Tampa, FL	68.60
Nogales, AZ	68.19
San Ysidro, CA	59.10
Houston, TX	58.79

Source: National Drug Intelligence Center, "National Drug Threat Assessment, 2006." January 2006.

- The global cultivation of opium poppies increased by 16 percent in 2004.

- Poppy cultivation in Colombia has decreased by two-thirds since 2001.

- The Center for Substance Abuse Treatment supports the certification and accreditation of over 1,000 heroin treatment programs that collectively treat over 200,000 patients annually.

- According to the Office of National Drug Control Policy, the number of admissions to treatment in which heroin was the primary drug of abuse increased from 216,452 in 1994 to 265,895 in 2004.

- According to the Office of National Drug Control Policy, the average age of those admitted to treatment for heroin during 2004 was 36.

- Heroin available in the U.S. is produced in four distinct geographical areas: South America (Colombia), Southeast Asia (primarily Burma), Mexico, and Southwest Asia (principally Afghanistan).

- According to the United States Sentencing Commission, between October 1, 2004 and January 11, 2005, there were 391 federal offenders sentenced for heroin-related charges in U.S. Courts.

Drug Prevention Stations in the United States

This map shows the major drug trafficking areas in the United States. High-Intensity Drug Trafficking Areas (HIDTA) works with local, state, and federal law enforcement agencies to combat trafficking. The program provides departments with technology, equipment, training, coordination, and leadership. Almost 9 percent of law enforcement agencies report that heroin is their biggest drug threat.

Source: Office of National Drug Control Policy, "High-Intensity Drug Trafficking Areas," www.whitehousedrugpolicy.gov.

43

Decline in Global Opium Poppy Cultivation

The cultivation of opium poppies (the flowers used to make heroin) has declined since the 1990s. This is due, in part, to multinational efforts to disrupt and end the production of heroin. This graph shows the number of opium fields, measured in hectares, in producing countries. One hectare is equal to 10 thousand square meters.

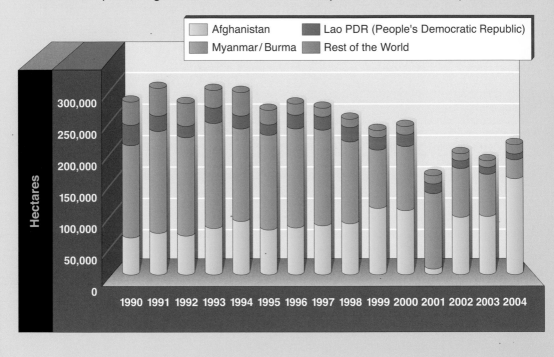

Source: United Nations Office on Drugs and Crime, "2005 World Drug Report," 2005.

- The U.N. Office on Drugs and Crime reported that opium production in Afghanistan increased by 64 percent in 2004.

Are Treatments for Heroin Addiction Effective?

> **Science has taught us that when medication treatment is integrated with other supportive services, patients are often able to stop heroin (or other opiate) use.**
>
> —National Institute on Drug Abuse, "Infofacts: Heroin," April 2006.

Treatment for heroin addiction is a mixed bag. People who want to stop using heroin have several options; however, none of them is 100 percent effective. These treatments include the use of other drugs (legal and prescribed by doctors), counseling, self-help groups, and hospitalization. As long as heroin addiction remains a serious problem, ways to treat the addiction will continue to be developed and evaluated.

Detoxification and Its Effects

The most basic method of treating heroin addiction is detoxification, which is the removal of heroin from the body. This is accomplished by the addict either gradually taking smaller amounts of heroin or by going "cold turkey" (stopping heroin use abruptly). Depending on how long the detoxification process takes, the addict can experience severe withdrawal symptoms. These symptoms include insomnia, restlessness, and vomiting. In general the symptoms emerge between two to three days after the most recent use of heroin and last several days. For many addicts, the pain of withdrawal symptoms is too excruciating to bear and they find that symptoms can only be relieved by turning again to heroin.

Using Methadone and Other Drugs to Treat Addiction

The pains of withdrawal are why treatments that combine detoxification with drugs that help ease withdrawal symptoms have become one of the most popular ways to treat heroin addiction. Methadone is the best known of these drugs. German scientists developed methadone, a synthetic opiate, in the late 1930s in an effort to discover drugs that would serve as analgesics without being addictive, unlike morphine. In the 1940s researchers in England found that morphine addicts responded positively to doses of methadone. As heroin gradually became more popular than morphine among opiate addicts, research started to focus on whether methadone could also end dependence on heroin. Methadone emerged as a treatment for heroin addiction in the 1970s.

> The most basic method of treating heroin addiction is detoxification, which is the removal of heroin from the body.

Heroin addicts take methadone in one of three ways, all orally: as a tablet dissolved in water, as a powder dissolved in water, or in liquid form. Regardless of which method a methadone user chooses, the dose will ease the withdrawal symptoms of heroin addiction for 24 hours. Methadone also lessens the physical cravings for heroin and blocks the effects of heroin should an addict use it despite being on methadone.

The benefits of methadone have been well documented. According to statistics from the National Institute on Drug Abuse, criminal activity among addicts treated with methadone is 53 percent lower than when they used heroin, while full-time employment in that group has increased by 24 percent.

Although it is relatively effective, methadone can be inconvenient. Because the effects of methadone last only 20 to 24 hours and because it is a very addictive drug if not properly monitored, addicts on methadone must take the drug every day at a clinic, where a doctor distributes it. Methadone users can also experience uncomfortable physical side effects, such as nausea, constipation, and respiratory problems. Alternatives have emerged in recent years that are more accessible and require less frequent use. Levomethadyl is taken every three days; however, its use has been limited by studies that show it can cause heart problems. Another drug that helps treat heroin addiction is buprenorphine, a pill that is available at pharmacies with a prescription. Its users are less physically dependent on their treatment than addicts who take methadone because it can be taken as infrequently as every three days and because its users experience fewer withdrawal symptoms. A third option is naltrexone or naloxone, which are used with the other drugs to help counteract the effects of heroin if the addict continues to use it.

Reducing the Harm of Heroin Addiction

Another way to treat heroin addiction is by acknowledging that some addicts might never be able to end their dependence and focusing on ensuring that they are able to protect themselves from heroin's dangerous physical effects. This approach is known as harm reduction. Syringe exchange programs (SEPs) are an example of a harm reduction policy. In these programs, addicts trade in used syringes for sterile ones. The theory behind these programs is to reduce the spread of diseases such as AIDS and hepatitis, which are transmitted through the sharing of dirty syringes. As of August 2006 185 needle exchange programs are operating in the United States, despite the fact that the federal government has not provided any funding for them since 1989. The programs have met with opposition from many politicians and critics, who charge that the government should not be

> " Criminal activity among addicts treated with methadone is 53 percent lower than when they used heroin. "

in the business of giving addicts needles and who also argue that these programs encourage drug use. However, as one doctor asserts, "Critics have questioned whether SEPs might increase illicit drug use, disease spread, or the number of used syringes in public places. Abundant data are available to alleviate these concerns. Numerous studies have shown that SEPs do not increase drug use, the number of IDUs [injection drug users], or the problem of discarded syringes."[12]

An unusual harm reduction program is available in England, Switzerland, and the Netherlands. All three nations allow addicts to receive heroin by prescription. The World Health Organization (WHO) conducted a study in 1998 to determine whether giving addicts heroin would be beneficial and concluded that such programs reduce crime and make the public more knowledgeable about heroin addiction. Another advantage of these programs is that the supply of heroin in clinics is safer and its purity more consistent than what is available on the streets; consequently, addicts can be certain that they will not receive a deadly amount. Despite concerns that prescribing heroin might encourage drug addiction, a study in the medical journal *Lancet* concluded that heroin use has remained stable in Switzerland since 1994. In England, however, heroin prescription has led to as much as a 30 percent annual increase in heroin use, according to the U.S. Drug Enforcement Administration.

Prescribing heroin by itself is no guarantee that an addict will be able to minimize the harm associated with his or her habit; however, studies have shown that prescribing heroin and methadone together is more effective in reducing many of the problems related to heroin addiction, than just prescribing methadone. Researchers in the Netherlands conducted a study on the effectiveness of coprescribing heroin and methadone. They found that providing both drugs to addicts helped reduce the physical, social, and mental problems of addiction and concluded that coprescriptions were just as safe as prescribing only methadone; however, because the study was limited to addicts who were resistant to treatment, it is uncertain whether all heroin addicts would benefit from coprescriptions.

> " In England, . . . heroin prescription has led to as much as a 30 percent annual increase in heroin use, according to the U.S. Drug Enforcement Administration. "

Counseling and Rehabilitation

Methadone and other drugs are not necessarily the best treatment for heroin addiction, because they do not help addicts cope with the emotional cravings for heroin. In these cases, heroin addicts are often better served by participating in self-help programs such as Narcotics Anonymous, entering rehabilitation centers, or undergoing behavioral therapy. These treatments help heroin users by giving them an opportunity to talk to people in similar situations or to people who have the knowledge to help addicts end their drug use.

"Twelve-step programs," popularized by Alcoholics Anonymous (AA), are a common way to fight a variety of addictions. Participants meet regularly to discuss their struggles and triumphs. Narcotics Anonymous (NA), an offshoot of AA, is the most well known of the twelve-step programs that target drug abuse; another one is Recoveries Anonymous. A survey conducted by NA reported that the average participant has been drug free for 7.4 years. As of 2005 more than

> **The first drug court was established in 1989, and more than 400,000 people have participated in a drug court program since then.**

33,000 meetings were being held each week in 116 nations. Other, non-religiously based twelve-step programs are available as well. Alternatives to Narcotics Anonymous and the twelve-step method, such as SMART (Self-Management and Recovery Training) and Rational Recovery (which does not utilize group meetings), have also been established.

Other options exist for addicts whose problems cannot be solved with self-help groups. Long-term residential care in rehabilitation centers is geared toward people with a lengthy history of heroin use who need a greater amount of counseling and medical care in order to learn how to live drug free. Addicts with a less serious dependency can opt for inpatient programs, which run between three and six weeks on average, or outpatient programs, which do not require a stay at a hospital or rehabilitation center. All of these treatments can also be geared toward teenagers.

Drug Courts

A drug court, as defined by the National Association of Drug Court Professionals, "is a special court given the responsibility to handle cases involving substance-abusing offenders through comprehensive supervision, drug testing, treatment services and immediate sanctions and incentives."[13] The first drug court was established in 1989, and more than 400,000 people have participated in a drug court program since then. Drug courts help reduce the number of addicts who are repeatedly arrested for possession. Participants are expected to complete a one-year treatment program and sometimes meet other requirements, such as remaining free of heroin or holding a job. Drug-related charges are dropped after successful completion of the program. Participants who do not finish the program may be sentenced to jail. As of September 2004, seventeen hundred drug courts were either planned or in operation. The General Accounting Office reports that between 36 and 60 percent of participants complete their program and that they are 10 to 30 percent less likely to be rearrested than drug users who do not enter a drug court program.

The many types of drug treatment available show that if heroin addicts are committed to conquering their problem, they can find a way to do so. Ending an addiction to heroin can be difficult and may take repeated attempts, but doing so improves not only the lives of the former addicts but society as a whole.

Are Treatments for Heroin Addiction Effective?

"LAAM [levomethadyl] may be a valuable complement to methadone in some cases. Recent research has shown the advantages of including LAAM in a methadone maintenance regimen."

—Douglas Longshore et al., "Levo-alpha-acetylmethadol (LAAM) Versus Methadone: Treatment Retention and Opiate Use," *Addiction*, 2005.

Longshore was the associate director at the University of California at Los Angeles Integrated Substance Abuse Programs (ISAP); Jeffrey Annon is the chairperson of the National Institute on Drug Abuse Clinical Trials Network; M. Douglas Anglin is a researcher at the ISAP; and Richard A. Rawson is an associate director at ISAP.

"Methadone is not a cure for the problem of opioid dependency. It is a treatment—and one that is effective for only as long as a person continues to take it appropriately."

—Holly Catania, *About Methadone*, Drug Policy Alliance, 2006. www.dpf.org.

Catania is a consultant for the International Harm Reduction Development Program and the project director for the International Center for Advancement of Addiction Treatment.

* Editor's Note: While the definition of a primary source can be narrowly or broadly defined, for the purposes of Compact Research, a primary source consists of: 1) results of original research presented by an organization or researcher; 2) eyewitness accounts of events, personal experience, or work experience; 3) first-person editorials offering pundits' opinions; 4) government officials presenting political plans and/or policies; 5) representatives of organizations presenting testimony or policy.

❝In my opinion methadone is not the answer. Spend the money on opening a detox facility, . . . as well as more treatment facilities [and] recovery homes.❞

—I.E. Hawksworth, "Former Addict Says Methadone Not the Answer," *Abbotsford Times,* February 22, 2003.

Hawksworth is a former heroin addict who works with imprisoned heroin addicts.

❝Many methadone-maintained patients are able to secure and maintain gainful employment, remain heroin-free, improve health and reduce the risk of exposure to HIV/AIDS.❞

—Connecticut Clearinghouse, "Heroin Use and Methadone Treatment," August 2000. www.ctclearinghouse.org.

The Connecticut Clearinghouse is a library and resource center funded by the Department of Mental Health and Addiction Services.

❝By giving addicts a sustained period of sobriety and the tools to help maintain that sobriety, drug courts also save money that would otherwise be spent on health care, prisons and law enforcement.❞

—Peter Anderson, "Treatment with Teeth," *American Prospect,* December 2003.

Anderson is a drug court judge.

66 **Drug Courts are creating a separate system of justice for drug offenders, . . . where the defense, prosecution and judge work as a team to force the offender into a treatment program.** 99

—Douglas A. McVay, "Drug Courts and Treatment as an Alternative to Incarceration,"
Common Sense for Drug Policy. February 2006. www.csdp.org.

McVay is the director of research at Common Sense for Drug Policy, an organization that is dedicated to reforming drug policy and promoting harm reduction programs.

66 **Drug courts not only don't accomplish their goals but they may be widening the criminal justice net . . . [and] taking treatment slots away from voluntary, community-based programs.** 99

—Melissa Hostetler, "Rethinking Drug Courts," *Clamor,* March/April 2002.

Hostetler is a journalist.

66 **[Methadone] treatment supplemented with heroin improves the physical, mental, and social functioning of heroin addicts.** 99

—Marcel G. W. Dijkgraaf et al., "Cost Utility Analysis of Co-Prescribed Heroin Compared with Methadone Maintenance Treatment in Heroin Addicts in Two Randomised Trials," *British Medical Journal,* June 4, 2005.

Dijkgraaf led a team of Dutch researchers and professors studying the effectiveness of treating heroin addicts with a combination of methadone and heroin.

66 **Many needle exchange programs do not make any serious effort to treat drug addiction.** 99

—David S. Noffs, "Should Needle Exchange Be Publicly Funded?" *Close to Home Online,* www.pbs.org.

Noffs is a former president of Drug Watch International.

....

66 **Syringe prescription is an extremely effective way to address the need of IDUs [intravenous drug users] to gain increased access to both syringes and health care.** 99

—Josiah D. Rich, "Prescribing Syringes to Injection Drug Users: What the Family Physician Should Know," *American Family Physician,* July 1, 2003.

Rich is a professor of medicine and community health at Brown University.

....

66 **A basic tenet of harm reduction is that there has never been, is not now, and never will be a drug-free society.** 99

--Drug Policy Alliance, "Reducing Harm: Treatment and Beyond," www.drugpolicy.org.

The Drug Policy Alliance is an organization that seeks to end the war on drugs.

....

66 **Both behavioral and pharmacological treatments help . . . [increase] employment rates and lower risk of HIV and other diseases and criminal behavior.** 99

—National Institute on Drug Abuse, "Research Report: Heroin—Abuse and Addiction," May 2005. www.nida.nih.gov.

NIDA supports research on heroin addiction.

....

66 The truth which has been trampled under the cavalry of the drug warriors is that, properly prescribed, pure heroin is a benign drug. **99**

—Nick Davies, "Make Heroin Legal," *Guardian,* June 14, 2001.

Davies is a writer for the Manchester, England, newspaper the *Guardian*.

Are Treatments for Heroin Addiction Effective?

- Two hundred eighty-one thousand Americans received treatment for heroin addiction in 2003.

- Forty percent of heroin addicts admitted for treatment were given methadone.

- The relapse rate of drug court participants two years after graduation is 27.5 percent.

- Incarcerating a drug offender costs between $20,000 and $50,000 per year. By comparison, placing an offender in a drug court program costs between $2,500 and $4,000 annually.

- Needle exchange programs are available in 36 states and the District of Columbia.

- A clean syringe costs ten cents.

- Needle exchange programs reduce the rate of HIV infections by 11 percent.

- Forty-eight states permit over-the-counter sales of syringes.

- Buprenorphine, a medication used to treat heroin addiction, was created in England in 1969.

Drug Courts in the United States

Drug courts are designed to reduce the number of addicts who are repeatedly arrested on drug charges. They are given the responsibility to handle cases uniquely by supervising, testing, counseling, and monitoring addicts. Between 36 and 60 percent of participants complete the programs and are 10 to 30 percent less likely to be rearrested than drug users who do not enter a drug court program.

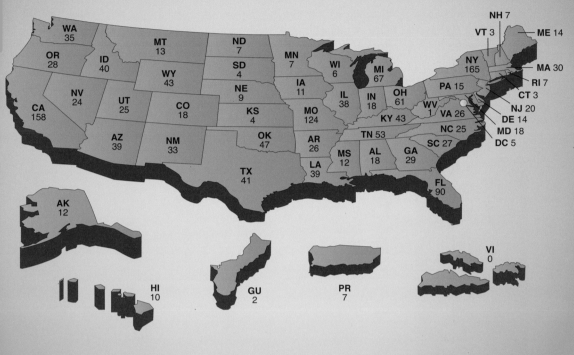

Source: National Drug Institute, "Painting the Current Picture: A National Report Card on Drug Courts and Other Problem Solving Court Programs in the United States," vol. I, no. 2, May 2005.

- Criminal activity among former heroin users who are in methadone treatment has decreased by more than 53 percent.

- According to SAMSA, heroin admissions represented 13 percent of the total drug/alcohol admissions for treatment during 1994 and 14.2 percent of the treatment admissions in 2004.

- According to NIDA, methadone, a medication that blocks the effects of heroin, has a proven treatment record when prescribed at a high enough dosage level for people addicted to heroin.

Using Other Drugs to Reduce Cravings and Withdrawal Symptoms

Buprenorphine-naloxone and buprenorphine alone both reduce the craving heroin addicts experience when not using the drug. These drugs are also administered to reduce withdrawal symptoms, which include insomnia, vomiting, restlessness, sweating, chills, and fever. A placebo is a harmless sugar pill used in medical trials to help measure the effect of a test drug.

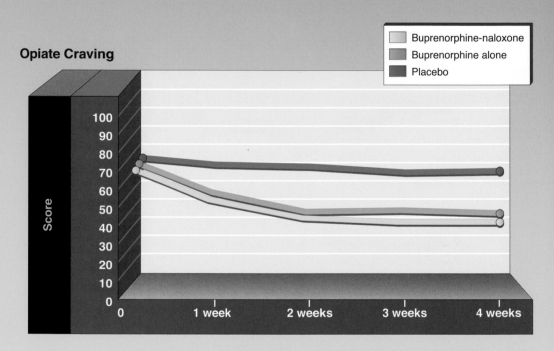

Opiate Craving

Source: National Institute on Drug Abuse, "Successful Trial Caps 25-Year Buprenorphine Development Effort," September 2004.

- Buprenorphin, naloxone, and naltrexone are medications that are approved by the FDA to treat heroin addiction.

- The initial symptoms of heroin withdrawal may include sweats, cramping, constipation, and anxiety or can be as medically complex as seizures, convulsions, and delirium tremors.

- Heroin use has doubled in Massachusetts over the past 10 years.

- According to the DEA approximately 1.2 percent of the population reported heroin use at least once in their lifetime.

- According to NIDA, primary heroin treatment admissions ranged from 62 to 82 percent of all illicit drug admissions in Baltimore, Boston, and Newark.

Methadone Is an Effective Treatment

This graph shows the decline in heroin use among addicts who undergo different types of treatment: methadone treatment, clinic treatment, or a combination of both. Addicts who relied solely on methadone had used heroin an average of 27.6 days during the previous month. One year after beginning treatment, they were averaging only 5.8 days of use per month. By comparison, although addicts who visited a clinic or utilized both treatments used heroin less frequently prior to receiving treatment, after one year they were using heroin as frequently as methadone-only addicts.

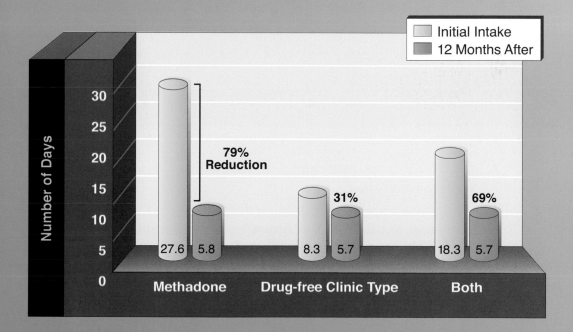

Source: Jeanette L. Johnston et al., "The Baltimore Drug and Alcohol Treatment Outcomes Study," January 2002. Reprinted in "America's Heroin Crisis, Colombian Heroin, and How We Can Improve Plan Columbia," hearing before the Committee on Government Reform, December 12, 2002.

Ages of Heroin Users in Treatment

This table shows the age breakdown of heroin users in treatment programs. According to the table, the number of addicts in treatment who were between the ages of twenty-five and thirty-four decreased significantly between 1992 and 2000, while all other age groups experienced a rise in admissions.

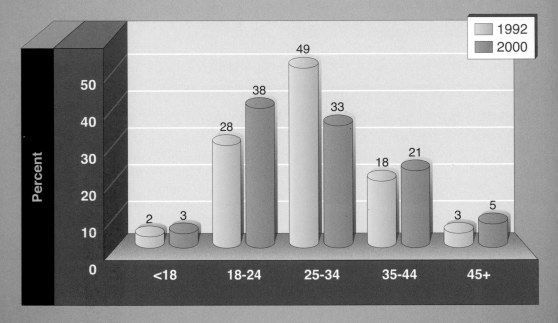

Source: Drug and Alcohol Services Information System, "New Heroin Users Admitted to Treatment: 1992-2000" DADIS Report, October 10, 2003.

- Current estimates suggest that nearly 600,000 people need treatment for heroin addiction.

- According to the Drug and Alcohol Services Information System, heroin and other opiates accounted for 77 percent of all treatment admissions for injection drug abuse in 2003.

Should Heroin Use Be Decriminalized or Legalized?

> **Reformers are as eager as ever to debate the efficacy of the drug laws, while supporters of the drug war discuss the issue only grudgingly.**
>
> —Timothy Lynch, *After Prohibition*, 2000.

For the most part, discussions on the best ways to prevent and treat heroin addiction are largely free of controversy. One debate that has created strong feelings is whether heroin use should be decriminalized or legalized. Decriminalization would allow an individual to possess a small amount of the drug without criminal penalties. Legalizing heroin would permit the sale of heroin on the open market, most likely under the same restrictions that govern alcohol and tobacco sales, such as banning the sale of heroin to minors. Although the decriminalization and legalization of heroin do not mean the same thing, they both treat the use of heroin as a largely personal decision that should not be the concern of the government.

Reducing the Legal Penalties of Heroin Use

Advocates for changing the way that heroin is handled by law enforcement have several arguments for why people who use heroin should not be fined or incarcerated. One view is that if they are not treated like criminals, users might feel more comfortable about seeking treatment or counseling if they become addicted. Supporters of decriminalization also contend that lifting the criminal penalties for heroin possession would enable state and federal governments to free the court systems and jails for more serious crimes. The more controversial proposal of legalizing heroin could benefit society, its supporters argue, by reducing crime—first, because selling heroin would no longer be illegal and second, because legalization would eliminate the violent crime that often accompanies drug dealing. Heroin would also meet government standards for purity and therefore be made safer. Heroin sold legally would not be laced with fentanyl or other deadly drugs.

> **Portugal decriminalized heroin possession in July 2001.**

Heroin decriminalization and legalization has already occurred in several countries. The drug is legally available to addicts in Switzerland. Portugal decriminalized heroin possession in July 2001. Instead of jail time, a Portuguese person found carrying heroin might be fined, ordered to perform community service, or placed in a rehab program. Heroin users in the Netherlands are also placed in rehabilitation instead of jail. The Netherlands ranks lower in the proportionate number of heroin users than many other Western European nations, and heroin-related deaths in that country dropped by 40 percent between the late 1970s and late 1990s. Mexico's congress approved a bill in April 2006 that would decriminalize the personal possession of small amounts of heroin, cocaine, marijuana, and ecstasy; however, pressure from the U.S. State Department and the mayors of U.S. border cities concerned that such a law could increase drug use in their municipalities make it unlikely that a decriminalization bill would have enough votes to override a veto by Mexico's president.

Selling Opium Legally

A different approach to heroin legalization is to permit Afghanistan to sell opium legally. The opium could then be used to produce painkillers for Third World nations who could not otherwise afford such medications. Maia Szalavitz, a journalist who writes about health and public policy issues, argues that legalizing opium "would improve the Afghan economy, deprive terrorists of income and keep heroin away from dealers and addicts."[14] According to Szalavitz, the United States would save $180 million per year compared to the cost of eradicating Afghanistan's poppy crops ($600 million versus $780 million) if it bought all of Afghanistan's poppies for the same price that drug lords pay.

Decriminalization Versus the War on Drugs

Decriminalizing or legalizing heroin would send a message that America's War on Drugs—at the very least, the war on heroin—has been a failure. The U.S. government spends $20 billion each year to prevent the distribution of drugs. Many critics charge that the so-called war has not only failed to reduce drug use but has also increased crime and corruption. Norm Stamper, a former Seattle police chief, argues, "The United States has, through its war on drugs, fostered political instability, official corruption, and health and environmental disasters around the globe. In truth, the U.S.-sponsored international 'War on Drugs' is a war on poor people."[15] He also points to studies that indicate property crime would be lowered by as much as 50 percent if drugs were decriminalized because heroin users would not have to commit crimes to pay for their addictions. Stamper is not alone in being a police officer who believes heroin laws should be relaxed. The Association of Chief Police Officers, a British organization, called for the legalization of heroin in December 2001 because doing so would eliminate the multibillion-dollar criminal conspiracy that controls the heroin trade.

> " **Critics of current drug laws contend that these laws disproportionately target African Americans.** "

Another argument in favor of legalizing heroin is that doing so could benefit minorities. Critics of current drug laws contend that these laws disproportionately target African Americans. According to the Leadership Council on Civil Rights, "Blacks are just 12 percent of the population and 13 percent of the drug users . . . [but] blacks are 38 percent of those arrested for drug offenses and 59 percent of those convicted of drug offenses."[16] In addition, the crimes associated with drugs often occur in urban areas. Therefore, decriminalizing or legalizing heroin could make such neighborhoods safer.

Decriminalization Harms Children and Adults

Decriminalizing or legalizing heroin could be harmful to children. Changing the legal status of heroin may make it more available to the children of drug abusers, particularly if heroin is used inside the home. Peter de Marneffe, an associate professor of philosophy at Arizona State University, writes: "A general increase in the availability of heroin would therefore increase the risk to children of inadequate parenting, and would make it more likely that young persons disposed to drug abuse will not do what they need to do in order to get a decent education [and] develop good work habits."[17] Allowing people to possess small amounts of heroin could also send the message to children that drug use is acceptable. Furthermore, just as many adolescents steal cigarettes from their parents or sneak alcohol when they are not being watched, they will also be more able to use heroin if it is legal for their parents to keep it in the house. Teenagers may also acquire fake IDs if only legal adults can purchase heroin.

> **Heroin legalization ignores the other problems facing the poor, such as the lack of a quality education.**

Decriminalization and legalization could also result in higher rates of addiction and subsequent problems related to the increased number of addicts. The Drug Enforcement Administration, in its publication *Speaking Out Against Drug Legalization,* writes, "Legalization would significantly increase drug use and addiction—and all the social costs that go with it."[18] The DEA suggests that legalizing drugs could lead to decreased worker productivity, an increase in traffic fatalities, and a greater economic burden on the health-care system.

A further argument against eliminating the criminal penalties for heroin sale and possession is that doing so could devastate poorer neighborhoods. Katie Grant, writing for the weekly British magazine the *Spectator*, suggests that even if heroin is legalized, drug dealers will continue to target impoverished people who may not be able to afford the price of legal drugs. She also argues that heroin legalization ignores the other problems facing the poor, such as the lack of a quality education. Grant concludes, "Although our world is run by the middle classes, it is those whose lot in life is rather less comfortable who would bear the real brunt of moves towards the legalisation of hard drugs."[19]

Reducing Criminal Penalties

The solution to the debate on changing the criminal penalties for heroin may well be a compromise: keeping heroin illegal while setting less harsh criminal penalties. De Marneffe suggests eliminating prison terms for first or second offenses, as long as the defendant completes probation successfully. Increasing the use of drug courts, where people convicted of heroin possession are given rehabilitation instead of jail sentences, is another option.

American policies governing heroin are not likely to change quickly. The efforts made in other nations to relax the penalties for heroin sales and possession, however, suggest that the United States may follow suit if the decriminalization and legalization of heroin are shown to not increase the rates of addiction or crime.

Should Heroin Use Be Decriminalized or Legalized?

❝The drug war doesn't fight crime; it fuels crime.❞

—Robert Sharpe, "U.S. Should Follow Europe's Lead in Drug Law Reform," *Long Island Newsday,* January 3, 2001.

Sharpe is a program officer with the Lindesmith Center-Drug Policy Foundation.

....

❝It is the U.S.'s prohibition of [illegal] drugs that has spawned an ever-expanding international industry of torture, murder and corruption.❞

—Norm Stamper, "How Legalizing Drugs Will End the Violence," July 28, 2006. www.alternet.com.

Stamper is a former chief of the Seattle Police Department.

....

* Editor's Note: While the definition of a primary source can be narrowly or broadly defined, for the purposes of Compact Research, a primary source consists of: 1) results of original research presented by an organization or researcher; 2) eyewitness accounts of events, personal experience, or work experience; 3) first-person editorials offering pundits' opinions; 4) government officials presenting political plans and/or policies; 5) representatives of organizations presenting testimony or policy.

❝ If heroin and cocaine were legalised for adults, it would be easier for the police to concentrate their fire on . . . other criminal acts. ❞

—Bruce Anderson, "Dead Children Are Not Reliable Counsellors: It Is Time to Legalise Heroin," *Spectator,* March 9, 2002.

Anderson is a writer for the British magazine *Spectator.*

❝ 120 years ago, heroin and cocaine were legal and plentiful. What was the result? Addiction and crime problems were at an unprecedented high level. ❞

—Asa Hutchinson, "The Past, Present, & Future of the War on Drugs," November 15, 2001. www.dea.gov.

Hutchinson is a former administrator of the Drug Enforcement Administration.

❝ Britain, which has had a relatively liberal approach to the prescribing of opiate drugs to addicts since 1928 . . . has seen an explosive increase in addiction to opiates. ❞

—Theodore Dalrymple, "Don't Legalize Drugs," *City Journal,* Spring 1997.

Dalrymple is a doctor and a writer for publications such as *City Journal* and *Spectator.*

❝ Legalization of cocaine, marijuana, and heroin would lead to large reductions in drug-related crime and mortality, but also to large increases in drug use and addiction. ❞

—Robert Maccoun and Peter Reuter, "Marijuana, Heroin, and Cocaine: The War on Drugs May Be a Disaster, but Do We Really Want a Legalized Peace?" *American Prospect,* June 3, 2002.

Maccoun and Reuter are professors of public policy.

❝ It is those whose lot in life is rather less comfortable who would bear the real brunt of moves towards the legalisation of hard drugs. ❞

—Katie Grant, "A Fix for the Middle Classes," *Spectator,* March 16, 2002.

Grant is a columnist for the British magazine *Spectator*.

···

❝ Legalization—and the increased addiction it would spawn—would result in lost workforce productivity. ❞

—Drug Enforcement Administration, *Speaking Out Against Drug Legalization,* May 2003. www.dea.gov.

The DEA enforces U.S. laws on controlled substances.

···

❝ Without prohibition, [heroin and other] drugs would sell for much, much less. They would not present any significant opportunity for terrorist groups to profit from their production or sale. ❞

—Eugene Oscapella, testimony before the Senate of Canada Special Committee on Illegal Drugs, Ottawa, Canada, October 29, 2001. www.cfdp.ca.

Oscapella is a lawyer and founding member of the Canadian Foundation for Drug Policy.

···

❝ Heroin brings pleasure and relief. We can therefore predict that adolescents in every economic group would begin using it regularly if it were legalized. ❞

—Peter de Marneffe, "Against the Legalization of Heroin," *Criminal Justice Ethics,* Winter/Spring 2003.

De Marneffe is an associate professor of philosophy at Arizona State University.

···

" History shows that, far from being a failure, drug-control programs are among the most successful public-policy efforts of the later half of the 20th century. **"**

—William J. Bennett, "The Bush Agenda," *Opinion Journal*, May 15, 2001.

Bennett was the director of the Office of National Drug Control Policy under President George H.W. Bush.

" More and more Americans are concluding that the drug war has been given a chance to work—and has failed. **"**

—Timothy Lynch, ed., *After Prohibition: An Adult Approach to Drug Policies in the 21st Century.* Washington, DC: Cato Institute, 2000.

Lynch is the director of the Cato Institute's project on criminal justice.

Facts and Illustrations

Should Heroin Use Be Decriminalized or Legalized?

- Drug-related crime cost the United States $107 billion in 2002.

- Eighty percent of drug arrests are for possession.

- The War on Drugs costs the U.S. federal government $20 billion per year.

- According to a 2002 study, 12.3 percent of drug users support the legalization of heroin.

- In 2006, Mexico's Congress approved a bill decriminalizing possession of small quantities of heroin for personal use.

- The retail value of the worldwide illegal drug market is $400 billion per year.

- Heroin deaths in the Netherlands, where the drug laws are more liberal than in the United States, decreased by 40 percent between the late 1970s and late 1990s.

- Studies indicate that property crime could be lowered by as much as 50 percent if drugs were decriminalized.

- When opium was legal in the United States in the 1880s, there were twice as many addicts as there are currently.

- According to the Office of National Drug Policy, more than 97 percent of the heroin-related cases in federal courts involve trafficking.

The History of Heroin/Opium Legalization

This graph suggests that the decision by the United States in 1924 to ban the distribution of heroin initially helped to reduce the number of addicts. The number has risen sharply since the 1940s, however, indicating that whether or not it is legal, heroin addiction remains a serious problem. Although the U.S. population has grown since World War II from 140 million to 300 million, that alone does not account for the exponential growth of heroin addiction during that period.

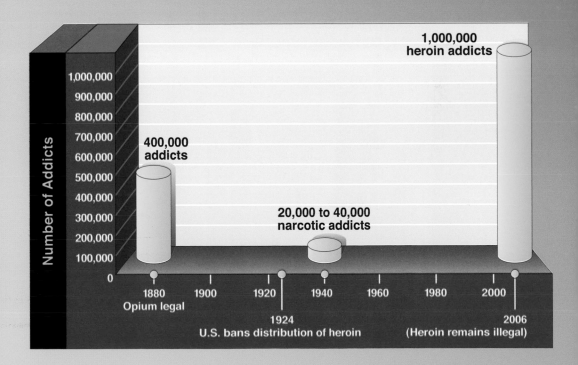

Source: U.S. Drug Enforcement Administration, *Speaking Out Against Drug Legalization.* National Institutes of Health, "Fact Sheet: Heroin Addiction," September 2006. www.dea.gov.

- The United Kingdom is one of the few countries where heroin is still available on prescription.

- According to the United Kingdom's Home Office, every £1 (U.S.$1.90) spent on drug treatment saves £3 (U.S. $5.70) in less crime.

United States Federal Spending on Drug Control

This graph shows how the federal government divides its drug control budget of about $12.6 billion. Domestic law enforcement and treatment make up more than half of the budget, while less money is spent on preventing drug use.

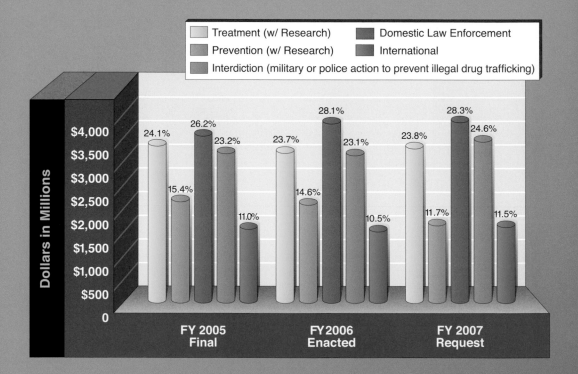

Source: National Drug Control Strategy, "FY 2007 Budget Summary," February 2006.

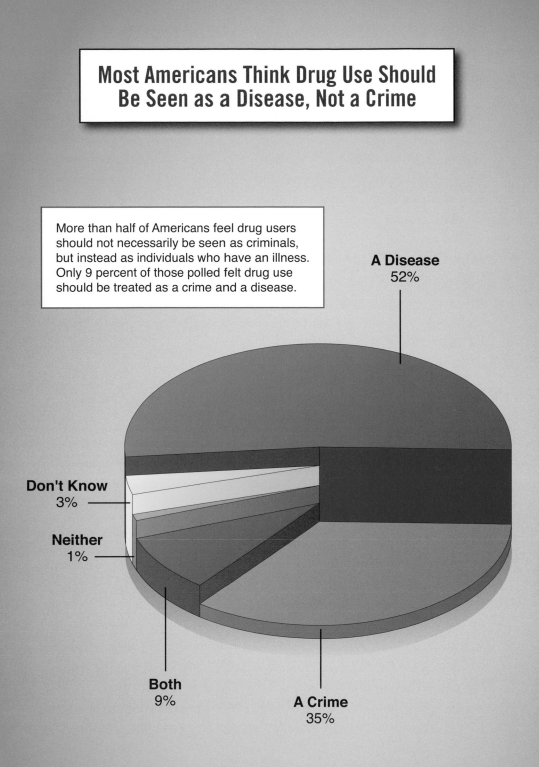

Most Americans Think Drug Use Should Be Seen as a Disease, Not a Crime

More than half of Americans feel drug users should not necessarily be seen as criminals, but instead as individuals who have an illness. Only 9 percent of those polled felt drug use should be treated as a crime and a disease.

A Disease
52%

Don't Know
3%

Neither
1%

Both
9%

A Crime
35%

Source: The Gallup Poll, May 2006. www.galluppoll.com.

Key People and Advocacy Groups

Bayer & Company: A pharmaceutical company founded in Germany in 1863, Bayer started producing and selling heroin in 1898, advertising it as a painkiller and cough suppressant. Bayer stopped producing heroin in 1913.

Max Bockmühl and Gustav Ehrhart: Bockmühl and Ehrhart were scientists at the I.G. Farbenkonzern pharmaceutical laboratories in Germany. They synthesized methadone in 1939. The drug, originally created as a substitute for morphine, has since proven to be an effective treatment for heroin addiction.

William S. Burroughs: Burroughs was a writer and one of the most famous heroin addicts of the twentieth century. His memoir *Junky*, published in 1953, detailed his drug use.

Thomas de Quincey: De Quincey was one of the first famous opium addicts. He was a nineteenth-century English essayist best known for writing *Confessions of an Opium Eater*, an 1822 essay that detailed his opium habit and the dreams he had while using the drug.

Vincent Dole: Dole was a doctor whose research proved that the cravings of heroin addicts can be reduced by giving them methadone. He also fought to keep methadone clinics open.

Heinrich Dreser: Dreser was a chemist who headed the pharmacological laboratory for the Bayer pharmaceutical company. He tested the painkilling and cough-suppressing properties of diacetylmorphine (later renamed heroin) on animals and some of his employees. Dreser's conclusion that heroin was safe and nonaddictive prompted Bayer to sell it commercially.

Narcotics Anonymous: Narcotics Anonymous, or NA, is an offshoot of Alcoholics Anonymous that was founded in the late 1940s. Its members meet to discuss their struggle to overcome addiction to heroin and other narcotics.

Friedrich Sertuerner: Sertuerner was a German scientist who created morphine in 1804 by dissolving opium in acid and adding ammonia. Morphine is needed to make heroin.

Lin Tse-hsu: Tse-hsu was an imperial Chinese commissioner who ordered foreign traders to surrender their opium in 1839. This action prompted the First and Second Opium Wars, both of which China lost, the first to Britain and the second to Britain and France.

C.R. Wright: The English researcher credited with discovering how to make heroin in 1874. He boiled morphine with the industrial acid acetic anhydride.

Chronology

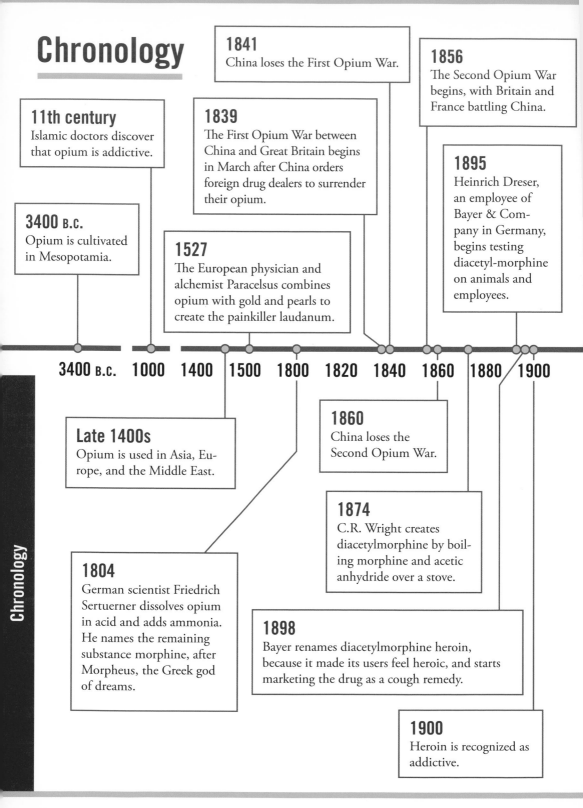

1841
China loses the First Opium War.

1856
The Second Opium War begins, with Britain and France battling China.

11th century
Islamic doctors discover that opium is addictive.

1839
The First Opium War between China and Great Britain begins in March after China orders foreign drug dealers to surrender their opium.

1895
Heinrich Dreser, an employee of Bayer & Company in Germany, begins testing diacetyl-morphine on animals and employees.

3400 B.C.
Opium is cultivated in Mesopotamia.

1527
The European physician and alchemist Paracelsus combines opium with gold and pearls to create the painkiller laudanum.

3400 B.C.   1000   1400   1500   1800   1820   1840   1860   1880   1900

Late 1400s
Opium is used in Asia, Europe, and the Middle East.

1860
China loses the Second Opium War.

1874
C.R. Wright creates diacetylmorphine by boiling morphine and acetic anhydride over a stove.

1804
German scientist Friedrich Sertuerner dissolves opium in acid and adds ammonia. He names the remaining substance morphine, after Morpheus, the Greek god of dreams.

1898
Bayer renames diacetylmorphine heroin, because it made its users feel heroic, and starts marketing the drug as a cough remedy.

1900
Heroin is recognized as addictive.

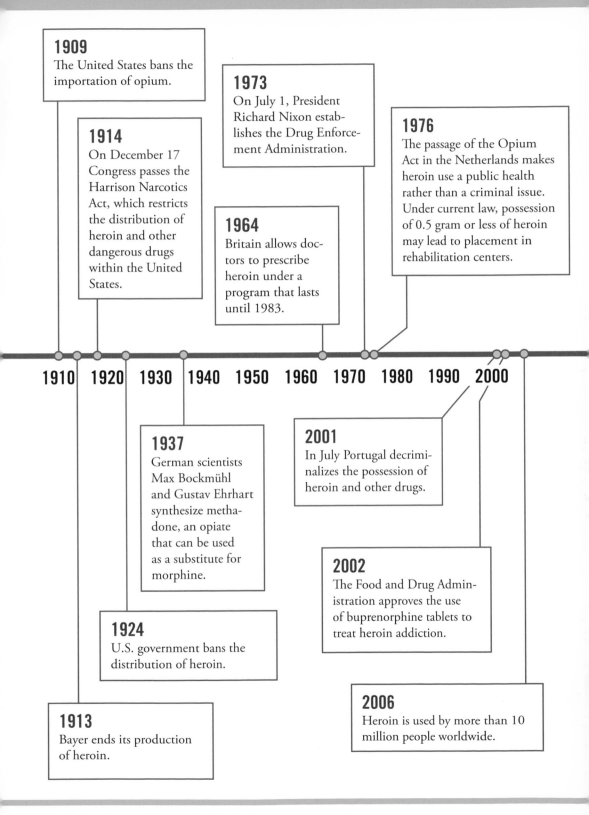

1909
The United States bans the importation of opium.

1914
On December 17 Congress passes the Harrison Narcotics Act, which restricts the distribution of heroin and other dangerous drugs within the United States.

1973
On July 1, President Richard Nixon establishes the Drug Enforcement Administration.

1964
Britain allows doctors to prescribe heroin under a program that lasts until 1983.

1976
The passage of the Opium Act in the Netherlands makes heroin use a public health rather than a criminal issue. Under current law, possession of 0.5 gram or less of heroin may lead to placement in rehabilitation centers.

1910 1920 1930 1940 1950 1960 1970 1980 1990 2000

1937
German scientists Max Bockmühl and Gustav Ehrhart synthesize methadone, an opiate that can be used as a substitute for morphine.

2001
In July Portugal decriminalizes the possession of heroin and other drugs.

2002
The Food and Drug Administration approves the use of buprenorphine tablets to treat heroin addiction.

1924
U.S. government bans the distribution of heroin.

1913
Bayer ends its production of heroin.

2006
Heroin is used by more than 10 million people worldwide.

Related Organizations

Canadian Centre on Substance Abuse (CCSA)

75 Albert St., Suite 300

Ottawa, ON

K1P 5E7, Canada

phone: (613) 235-4048

fax: (613) 235-8101

e-mail: info@ccsa.ca

Web site: www.ccsa.ca

The Canadian Centre on Substance Abuse (CCSA) is Canada's national drug abuse agency. It provides information and advice to help reduce the problems associated with substance abuse and addiction. CCSA publishes fact sheets, an annual report, and the quarterly newsletter *Action News.*

Common Sense for Drug Policy (CSDP)

1377-C Spencer Ave.

Lancaster, PA 17603

phone: (717) 299-0600

fax: (717) 393-4953

e-mail: info@csdp.org

Web site: www.csdp.org

CSDP is a nonprofit organization that aims to reform drug policy and expand public health measures—such as needle exchanges—that can reduce the health risks of heroin use. It supports the decriminalization of hard drugs, with such drugs becoming available only through prescription. The Web site provides links to reports and news stories about drug policies.

Do It Now Foundation

PO Box 27568

Tempe, AZ 85285-7568

phone: (480) 736-0599

fax: (480) 736-0771

Web site: www.doitnow.org

The mission of the Do It Now Foundation is to create and distribute accurate information on drugs and other health topics. The foundation also aims to monitor patterns in drug use and track developments in health research. It publishes pamphlets and booklets on heroin and other drugs.

Drug Enforcement Administration (DEA)

Mailstop: AES, 2401 Jefferson Davis Hwy.

Alexandria, VA 22301

phone: (202) 307-1000

Web site: www.dea.gov

The mission of the DEA is to enforce U.S. laws on controlled substances. In order to accomplish this goal, the DEA investigates drug traffickers and the criminals and gangs that distribute heroin and other illegal drugs. Its publications include the book *Get It Straight,* which provides teenagers with information on the dangers of drug abuse.

Drug Policy Alliance

70 West 36th St. 16th Floor,

New York, NY 10018

phone: (212) 613-8020

fax: (212) 613-8021

Web site: www.dpf.org

The Drug Policy Alliance is an organization that promotes alternatives to America's war on drugs. It promotes policies that reduce the harms of the prohibition and misuse of drugs and believes that people should not be punished for what they put into their own bodies. Publications on topics such as methadone are available on its Web site.

Narcotics Anonymous (NA)

PO Box 9999

Van Nuys, CA 91409

phone: (818) 773-9999

fax (818) 700-0700

e-mail: fsmail@na.org

Web site: www.na.org

Narcotics Anonymous is an international organization of recovering drug addicts. An offshoot of Alcoholics Anonymous, NA has chapters in 116 nations. The organization publishes books and pamphlets, the monthly *NA Way Magazine,* and annual conference reports.

National Center on Addiction and Substance Abuse at Columbia University (CASA)

633 Third Ave., 19th Floor

New York, NY 10017-6706

phone: (212) 841-5200

Web site: www.casacolumbia.org

CASA is a national organization that studies substance abuse, including heroin abuse. Its staff includes experts on addiction, public health, and criminology. CASA publishes newsletters and reports, including *National Survey of American Attitudes on Substance Abuse X: Teens and Parents.*

National Clearinghouse for Alcohol and Drug Information (NCADI)

PO Box 2345

Rockville, MD 20847-2345

phone: (800) 729-6686

fax: (240) 221-4292

Web site: www.health.org

NCADI is part of the federal government's Substance Abuse and Mental Health Services Administration. The clearinghouse provides information about preventing substance abuse and treating addictions. Its staff of specialists conducts searches and recommends appropriate print and video media. Publications, including "Tips for Teens: The Truth About Heroin," are also available on its Web site.

National Council on Alcoholism and Drug Dependence (NCADD)

22 Cortlandt St., Suite 801

New York, NY 10007-3128

phone: (212) 269-7797

fax: (212) 269-7510

e-mail: national@ncadd.org

Web site: www.ncadd.org

NCADD is a volunteer health organization that provides education and information on the prevention and treatment of alcoholism and drug addiction and advises the federal government on drug and alcohol policies. Publications are available for purchase from the site.

National Institute on Drug Abuse (NIDA)

National Institutes of Health

6001 Executive Blvd., Room 5213

Bethesda, MD 20892-9561

phone: (301) 443-1124

e-mail: information@nida.nih.gov

Web site: www.nida.nih.gov

NIDA is part of the National Institutes of Health. It supports more than 85 percent of the world's research on health issues relating to drug abuse and addiction, including heroin addiction. Its publications include *Research Report: Heroin Abuse and Addiction.*

Office of National Drug Control Policy (ONDCP)

Drug Policy Information Clearinghouse

PO Box 6000

Rockville, MD 20849-6000

phone: (800) 666-3332

fax: (301) 519-5212

Web site: www.whitehousedrugpolicy.gov

Part of the Executive Office of the President, the ONDCP establishes the goals, policies, and priorities of America's drug control program. The office aims to reduce the use, manufacturing, and trafficking of illegal drugs. It also seeks to reduce drug-related crime and health problems. Its Web site provides information on heroin.

Partnership for a Drug-Free America

405 Lexington Ave., Suite 1601

New York, NY 10174

(212) 922-1560

fax: (212) 922-1570

Web site: www.drugfree.org

The Partnership for a Drug-Free America is a nonprofit coalition of medical, health, communication, and educational professionals who work together to reduce the use of illegal drugs. The organization creates educational campaigns that teach people about the dangers of drugs. Information on illegal drugs, including personal stories of the effects heroin has on addicts and their families, is available on its Web site.

For Further Research

Books

Robert Ashton, *This Is Heroin.* London: Sanctuary, 2002.

Rachel Green Baldino, *Welcome to Methadonia: A Social Worker's Candid Account of Life in a Methadone Clinic.* Harrisburg, PA: White Hat Communications, 2001.

Karen Bellenir, ed., *Drug Information for Teens: Health Tips About the Physical and Mental Effects of Substance Abuse.* Detroit: Omnigraphics, 2002.

Jane Bingham, *Heroin: What's the Deal?* Portsmouth, NH: Heinemann, 2005.

Stacey L. Blachford and Kristine Krapp, eds., *Drugs and Controlled Substances: Information for Students.* Farmington Hills, MI: Gale, 2003.

David T. Courtwright, *Dark Paradise: A History of Opiate Addiction in America.* Cambridge, MA: Harvard University Press, 2001.

Alfred W. McCoy, *The Politics of Heroin: CIA Complicity in the Global Drug Trade, Afghanistan, Southeast Asia, Central America, Colombia.* Chicago: Lawrence Hills, 2003.

Joel Miller, *Bad Trip: How the War Against Drugs Is Destroying America.* Nashville: WND, 2004.

David F. Musto, ed., *One Hundred Years of Heroin.* Westport, CT: Auburn House, 2002.

James D. Orcutt and David R. Rudy, eds., *Drugs, Alcohol, and Social Problems.* Lanham, MD: Rowman & Littlefield, 2003.

Periodicals

Bruce Anderson, "Dead Children Are Not Reliable Counsellors: It Is Time to Legalise Heroin," *Spectator,* March 9, 2002.

Carolyn Bilsky, "Addicted to Heroin: One Survivor's Story," *Current Health 2,* December 2001.

John DiConsiglio, "Close-Up: Heroin," *Science World,* April 18, 2003.

———, "Hooked on Heroin," *Junior Scholastic,* April 25, 2003.

Economist, "The Afghan Plague," July 26, 2003.

Katie Grant, "A Fix for the Middle Classes," *Spectator,* March 16, 2002.

Melissa Hostetler, "Rethinking Drug Courts," *Clamor,* March/April 2002.

Donna Leinwand, "Heroin's Resurgence Closes Drug's Traditional Gender Gap," *USA Today,* May 9, 2000.

Alexia Lewnes, "The Downward Spiral Caused by a Drug Called Heroin," *Scholastic Choices,* November/December 2004.

Timothy Lynch, "War No More: The Folly and Futility of Drug Prohibition," *National Review,* February 5, 2001.

Robert Maccoun and Peter Reuter, "Marijuana, Heroin, and Cocaine: The War on Drugs May Be a Disaster, but Do We Really Want a Legalized Peace?" *American Prospect,* June 3, 2002.

Mike Males, "Raving Junk," *Extra!* December 2000.

Peter de Marneffe, "Against the Legalization of Heroin," *Criminal Justice Ethics,* Winter/Spring 2003.

Tim McGirk, "Terrorism's Harvest," *Time Asia,* August 2, 2004.

Sohail Abdul Nasir, "The Poppy Problem," *Bulletin of Atomic Scientists,* September/October 2004.

Evelyn Nieves, "Heroin, an Old Nemesis, Makes an Encore," *New York Times,* January 9, 2001.

Matthew Parris, "Yes, Heroin Can Kill, but the Doomsayers' Lies Are Just as Dangerous," *The Times* (London), February 5, 2005.

William Ratliff, "Colombia's Drug War Must Be Won in the U.S." *Los Angeles Times,* February 11, 2001.

Aram Roston, "Central Asia's Heroin Problem," *Nation,* March 25, 2002.

Philip Shiskin and David Crawford, "In Afghanistan, Heroin Trade Soars Despite U.S. Aid," *Wall Street Journal,* January 18, 2006.

John Sullivan, "It's Not the Heroin, It's the Needle," *New York Times,* January 11, 2004.

Jacob Sullum, "H: The Surprising Truth About Heroin and Addiction," *Reason,* June 2003.

U.S. News & World Report, "Struggling over a Policy Fix," June 6, 2005.

Robert Volkman, "Political Insanity About Marijuana and Drug Use," *Alternatives,* Fall 2004.

Internet Sources

Holly Catania, *About Methadone,* Drug Policy Alliance, 2006. www.dpf.org.

Central Intelligence Agency, "From Flowers to Heroin," March 2001. www.cia.gov.

National Clearinghouse for Alcohol and Drug Information, "Tips for Teens: The Truth About Heroin," April 2001. www.health.org.

National Institute on Drug Abuse, "InfoFacts: Heroin," April 2006. www.nida.nih.gov.

———, *Research Report: Heroin and Addiction,* May 2005. www.nida. nih.gov.

Jim Parker, "Heroin: The Junk Equation," Do It Now Foundation, September 2001. www.doitnow.org.

Substance Abuse and Mental Health Services Administration, "Planned Methadone Treatment for Heroin Admissions," June 13, 2003. www. oas.samhsa.gov.

Source Notes

Overview: The Scope of the Problem

1. "Opioids and Related Disorders," *Encyclopedia of Mental Disorders,* Farmington Hills, MI: Thomson Gale, 2005.
2. Thomas W. O'Connell, statement, hearing before the House Committee on International Relations, Afghanistan Drugs and Terrorism and U.S. Security Policy, 108th Cong., 2nd sess. February 12, 2004, p. 22.
3. Rogelio E. Guevara, statement, hearing before the House Committee on Government Reform, "America's Heroin Crisis, Colombian Heroin, and How We Can Improve Plan Colombia," 107th Cong, 2nd sess. December 12, 2002, p. 118.
4. Ian Vásquez, "The International War on Drugs," *Cato Handbook for Congress: Policy Recommendations for the 108th Congress,* Edward H. Crane and David Boaz, eds. Washington, DC: Cato Institute, 2003, p. 574.

How Dangerous Is Heroin?

5. James Tighe, "Drug Use and Addiction," British Broadcast Corporation, August 2006. www.bbc.co.uk.
6. Stanton Peele, "The Persistent, Dangerous Myth of Heroin Overdose," *Drug Policy Forum of Texas News,* August 1999.

How Can Heroin Use Be Prevented?

7. Drug Enforcement Administration, "DEA Mission Statement," www.dea.gov.
8. Dan Burton, statement, hearing before the House Committee on Government Reform, "America's Heroin Crisis, Colombian Heroin, and How We Can Improve Plan Colombia," 107th Cong, 2nd sess. December 12, 2002, p. 3.
9. Martin Fishbein et al., "Avoiding the Boomerang: Testing the Relative Effectiveness of Antidrug Public Service Announcements Before a National Campaign," *American Journal of Public Health,* February 2002.
10. Kendra Wright, "Dare We Admit It? Drug War Is a Bust with Our Children," *Oregonian,* January 20, 1998, p. E9.
11. Common Sense for Drug Policy, "The *Effective* National Drug Control Strategy, 1999." www.csdp.org.

Are Treatments for Heroin Addiction Effective?

12. Josiah D. Rich, "Prescribing Syringes to Injection Drug Users," *American Family Physician,* July 1, 2003.
13. National Association of Drug Court Professionals, "What Is a Drug Court?" www.nadcp.org.

Should Heroin Be Decriminalized or Legalized?

14. Maia Szalavitz, "Let a Thousand Licensed Poppies Bloom," *New York Times,* July 13, 2005.
15. Norm Stamper, "War on Crimes, Not on Drugs," Alternet, June 15, 2005. www.alternet.com.
16. Ronald Welch and Carlos T. Angulo, "Justice on Trial: Racial Disparities in

the American Criminal Justice System," Leadership Conference on Civil Rights, May 2000.

17. Peter de Marneffe, "Against the Legalization of Heroin," *Criminal Justice Ethics,* Winter/Spring 2003.

18. Drug Enforcement Administration, *Speaking Out Against Drug Legalization,* Washington, DC: Department of Justice, DEA, May 2003.

19. Katie Grant, "A Fix for the Middle Classes," *Spectator,* March 16, 2002.

List of Illustrations

List of Illustrations

Index

About the Author

San Diego resident Laura K. Egendorf received her B.A. in English from Wesleyan University. A book editor for the past nine years, she is especially interested in books that explore free speech or popular culture. When she is not working, Laura's interests include food, sports, music, and trivia.